American Diaries

JANEY G. BLUE

PEARL HARBOR, 1941

———◦◦◦◦———

by Kathleen Duey

———◦◦◦◦———

Aladdin Paperbacks

New York   London   Toronto   Sydne~

For Richard
For Ever

First Aladdin Paperbacks edition May 2001

Copyright © 2001 by Kathleen Duey

Aladdin Paperbacks
An imprint of Simon & Schuster
Children's Publishing Division
1230 Avenue of the Americas
New York, NY 10020

The text for this book was set in Fairfield Light.
Printed and bound in the United States of America

10 9 8 7 6 5 4 3 2

CIP data for this book is available
from the Library of Congress.

ISBN 0-689-84404-2

December 7, 1941, before dawn, Oahu, Hawaii:

I can hear Mrs. Fujiwara's roosters. They sound like Grandma's Rhode Island Reds on her place back home. Listening to them makes me homesick for Kansas every single morning. I am missing Tilly terribly right now, too. I'll probably never have a best friend again.

I heard Mom and Dad talking last night. I stood outside the kitchen door to eavesdrop—they are actually considering staying here. I am trying not to think about that very much.

Dad got up at 4:00 A.M. to go down to Hickam Airfield. Lieutenant Verst's jeep driver picked him up— they had some welding problem he had to solve. He went that early so he could be home in time to go fishing at 8:00 with Mr. Wilkins. Sunday is his only day to fish.

I don't have anything to do today. I wish I did.

I have been thinking about my name again.

Jane Blue . . .

Jane Blue. Janey Blue.

Janey G. Blue.

I like the way that sounds when I say it aloud.

Janey G. Blue

Mom will say it's silly to use my middle initial, that girls don't ever use initials, but I like it.

Jane Blue sounds completely ordinary. Plain Jane. And Janey Blue just sounds like some silly sixth grader—which is what I am, I suppose, but not forever. Janey G. Blue—now that sounds like someone I might want to be. Especially if no one ever finds out what the G. stands for. I love Grandma Gertrude, but her name is just too old-fashioned! I miss her more and more. And both my grandpas.

Oahu's palms and the beaches are more beautiful than any postcard could ever show. Our little town of Pearl City is swell too. We have a theater and a little store, and the streets are pretty, and there are lots of palm trees and banana trees and all kinds of other trees I don't know. In our backyard we have tangerines that are ripe right now. There are a few grand old houses—wealthy families built them for vacation homes, Mom said. But most of the houses are like ours—plain and nice enough.

I haven't made any friends yet. Mom says to be patient. These kids come from different backgrounds, she says. That's for sure.

Walking around in Honolulu for ten minutes, we see Chinese people and Japanese people and Filipinos and Portuguese and native Hawaiians, of course, and probably people from ten other places—more kinds of folks than Topeka, Kansas, will ever have, I bet.

In Pearl City there are mostly Chinese and

Japanese families with farms and fields of watercress or rice or taro or something. There are only two men like my father—metalworkers who came from somewhere in the United States to work on the military bases. Neither of the other two brought his wife or kids. Dad says a lot of the civilian pipe fitters left their families home. I wish we had stayed home. I miss Tilly most of all—but I even miss all my cousins, especially Norman and Carla.

I discovered something at school Friday: I hate poi. My parents and my mother's bridge club ladies have been trying to get me to taste it. It's purple and sticky, and it looks terrible, but I finally tried it. It tastes as awful as it looks. Mrs. Kaleiwahea at school says no special supper is complete without three-finger poi. You do eat it with your fingers—there is two-finger poi and three-finger poi, depending on how thick it is. Oh, well. I don't have to like it. Grandpa Ernst and Grandma Gertrude love sauerkraut—and nothing tastes and smells worse than that.

School at Sacred Heart is all right so far. I do love the music teacher, Miss Watanabe. She is so nice. Next year she will teach at a Japanese school—so I guess we are lucky to have her at Sacred Heart this year at all. Mary Frances and Lily Kaaloa and all the other girls who take piano lessons from Miss Watanabe think she is absolutely swell. When I grow up I want to be as pretty as she is—and have a singing voice as pure as hers.

Last night after the Christmas concert the grown-ups got going about the war again. Holy Golly, I am sick of hearing it. It's bad enough we have to listen to the planes from Hickam Field drill all the time. Some of the pilots pretend to be invading, and the others practice defending the harbor and the airfields, and they all pretend to fight. It's so noisy that Pokey hides under the bed.

Daddy thinks the Germans might manage to whip the British—and if that happens, he says America will have to get into the European war. Mr. Wilkins says the Japanese might end up attacking the United States, too, like they attacked China. And, he says, they might start with us—here in Hawaii, I mean. Daddy doesn't think so, though. I hope he's right.

I saw Miss Watanabe dodge inside the music room while they were talking. She was born in Honolulu and she is a very loyal American—she has a flag up in the music room! But she must hate hearing the men say "Japs" and all the other stuff they call the Japanese soldiers. I just hope the war stays far, far away from us.

CHAPTER ONE

Janey closed her diary and slid it onto her nightstand. Every time she thought about war, it made her stomach tighten. It made her want to go back to Kansas more than ever. She turned over to stare upward in the darkness. "I just wish I had a friend here I could talk to," she whispered.

At the foot of the bed, Pokey stirred. Janey felt the little terrier wriggle, stretch, then lie still again. Her breathing deepened, and Janey exhaled. The last thing she needed was for Pokey to wake up.

Mom and Dad had agreed to adopt Pokey—she had been left behind by the family that had moved out of their house. But it seemed like Pokey had adopted *them*—as though she was the one kind enough to let them live in *her* house. She was a little dog, a mixture of brown and black, with bright eyes. And she actually acted like she was listening sometimes. Janey blushed, remembering how she had told Pokey how homesick she was, how scared she was about the war spreading to include the United States. Pokey had tilted her head like Tilly always did, listening. Janey smiled in the dark. Tilly would be just plain insulted by that comparison.

It was true, though. Pokey kind of looked like her best friend, Tilly O'Neill, back in Kansas. It made a weird kind of sense, Janey thought. After all, Pokey was still her best friend here on Oahu. Her only friend, really.

Janey resisted an impulse to reach down and pat the little terrier. Waking Pokey up would mean getting up herself, and fast, before Pokey woke Mom and Michael up, too. One of the few things that Pokey insisted upon was being let out in the yard first thing in the morning—*her morning*. If Pokey wasn't let out immediately after she awakened, she'd glare at the back door and bark until someone opened it. It was funny, sometimes. Other times, when everyone just wanted to sleep in a little longer, it was awful.

Pokey stretched again. Janey tried to lie completely still, but her legs were in an awkward position, and it was hard to ignore her cramped muscles. She was glad it was Sunday. School was all right, but the nuns were really strict—it was sure different from her old school back in Topeka.

Janey hoped that later she and Mom and Michael could walk down and watch the people crabbing off the docks. Mom sometimes bought fresh crabs to cook. From the docks, they could see Hickam Field across the water, and a lot of the battleships. They were huge, like floating cities. Thousands of sailors lived on each one, her father had said. From the dock the sailors looked like seagulls in their white uniforms—scattered across the wide, tiered decks.

Just then, a familiar set of sounds came through Janey's closed bedroom door. First there was a floor creak, then her door jiggled on its hinges, a reaction to a door being opened down the hall. Then, Janey heard a quick patter of light footsteps. Michael was awake. And if her brother was up, no one would be sleeping in. Poor Mom. Sunday was the only day she ever got to sleep past six. Every other day of the week, Dad went to work early and she had to get up to make his breakfast.

"This is sure going to be a strange Christmas," Janey whispered to herself. Mr. Wilkins—the man Dad usually went fishing with—was from Toledo, Ohio. Since his wife hadn't come to Hawaii, he was going to have Christmas dinner with them. It would be odd to have no family members there—and a stranger instead.

"You awake, Janey?"

Some mornings, Janey pretended that she couldn't hear her little brother's breathy whisper on the other side of the door. But this morning, she sat up, startling Pokey into a blanket-tangling scramble.

"Janey?" Michael said a little louder.

"Come in, Michael," she called out.

The door opened slowly, and Janey saw her little brother's sleepy face in the light from the hall, his blond hair a ruff of silky curls around his head. Pokey scampered to the door and greeted Michael with a quick lick on the cheek, then wriggled past him to head for the back door. Janey heard her mother's footsteps follow Pokey's clicking nails.

"Janey?" Michael's voice was plaintive and wistful. "You're awake, aren't you?" He rubbed at his eyes.

"No," Janey said quietly.

"Yes, you are!" Michael whispered.

"Nope," Janey said firmly, careful not to move even an inch. "Jaaaneeeyyy!" Michael giggled.

Janey pretended to snore, taking long, shuddery breaths, then whooshing them out. Michael giggled again. Janey loved him. Other girls complained about little brothers, but Michael, at four, was completely adorable, except when he was crabby and tired—which wasn't too often. Still laughing, he played their usual game of closing the door, then opening it quickly, peering in to catch her with her eyes open.

"Come in," Janey relented, pushing down the covers so he could see that she was wide awake.

He smiled his sunny smile. "Daddy went to work," he told her, his eyes shining.

"I know. I hope he gets to fish later. If they go out in one of the Honolulu boats, maybe they can catch aku."

"Aku is good," Michael said, and the dreaminess in his voice made Janey smile. Before they had come to Hawaii, he had hated any kind of fish. Now he had a *favorite*!

Janey watched her brother crawl up to sit on the foot of her bed. His eyes went wide, and he touched the covers. "Pokey left her warm spot."

Janey smiled. "She always does. No matter how often I remind her to take it with her."

Michael giggled again.

"I'll take a quick bath before I make breakfast," Mom called from the hallway. She leaned through the door to smile at them. "Unless either of you is starving." She made a show of yawning and stretching. "Six o'clock! At least we all woke up," she added. "No one has to tiptoe around." She went off down the hall, and Janey heard the bathroom door open and close, then the sound of rushing water.

"NO ONE TIPTOES!" Michael yelled, rolling on the blankets. He shouted it over and over before Janey could hush him.

"The windows are wide open," Janey reminded him, and he quieted instantly, his hands over his mouth.

"Mrs. Fujiwara," he whispered, his eyes wide.

"I don't think she could have heard you," Janey fibbed because he looked so upset. Their neighbor scared her, too. Mrs. Fujiwara sometimes came walking across the road to ask them to keep their voices down as they played. She was always polite and never raised her own voice, but she never came across the road for any other reason. And she never smiled or looked a bit friendly. Every time she saw them, she frowned.

At first Janey had been glad about having another house right across the road. Because they lived on the edge of Pearl City, there were more fields than homes, and Janey had been excited the first time she'd noticed that Mrs. Fujiwara and her husband had a daughter about her age. But she hadn't yet managed even to introduce herself. Akiko was rarely outside unless she was on her way to school—or to work in the flooded taro field with her parents.

None of the Fujiwaras looked up or waved when Janey's father slowed the Buick passing them. Mom had offered to give them a ride into Honolulu whenever she went, but they seemed to prefer taking the train with all the other people who waited at the little depot in town.

"I wish they were nice," Janey said to Michael. He narrowed his eyes, and she reached out to smooth his hair, then realized her eyes were flooded. Michael saw her tears and wiped them off clumsily.

"It's just harder for me to have friends here than it was in Kansas," Janey explained, knowing that he wouldn't quite understand, but that he would listen. "It seems like everybody already has all the friends they need," she added. It was true. The girls who were friends at school had been friends since they were babies. And it seemed like the Hawaiian girls got along together, and the Japanese girls chose mostly Japanese friends . . . and so on. That narrowed things down and made it even harder.

"I want a best friend," Janey said aloud.

"I will be your best friend," Michael said quietly, and Janey knew he meant it with all his heart. She hugged him, then leaned back and swung her feet to the floor.

"Mrs. Fujiwara hates us," Michael said in a low voice.

Janey could only nod. Mrs. Fujiwara sure glared at them a lot. "Maybe. But Mom says if we just keep being polite, she will accept us eventually."

Michael was shaking his head. "I don't like her."

Janey leaned close to whisper, "I don't, either, really. But we still have to be polite."

Michael nodded solemnly. Janey smiled. He looked so serious sometimes, like an old man.

The sound of running water in the bathroom had stopped. Janey knew her mother loved to take baths here on Oahu. It was heaven to lie still in the deep tub, inhaling the sweet steam. Their water came from a spring up the road and it was different from any water she had ever tasted. But then, everything here was different.

"Let's go outside," Michael said.

Janey shook her head. "It's still dark out, silly."

Michael slid to the floor and crossed the room to look out her window. "Not for long. Hear the roosters?"

Janey smiled at him. "Go get dressed. I'll tie your shoes."

Michael nodded, then ran out of the room. Janey could hear the wooden floor creaking beneath his feet. This was an old house, but she liked it.

Janey got dressed, hesitating, then deciding to wear a navy skirt and white blouse. Her mother didn't approve of slacks unless they were going hiking in the mountains or on a picnic or something.

"I'm ready!" Michael sang out as he pounded back up the narrow hall. He skidded into her room and tripped over his shoelaces, falling sideways into the wall. He caught himself and careened toward Janey. She let him crash into her, bending just enough at the waist to absorb the shock. Then she hoisted him up onto her bed.

"You're getting heavy!"

"I'm growing fast," he agreed, repeating what their father said every time he picked Michael up.

Janey wished her father were home. This would be a perfect morning for a pillow fight or a game of tag. She got Michael settled on the bed, then bent to tie his shoes. When she straightened, she went to the window.

The moon was still up and nearly full. Janey framed her face with her hands to block out the reflection of the hall light and peered out. She could see the glitter of stars. No rain—at least for a few hours. Storms rolled in, then out, so quickly. Hawaii seemed to have rain nearly every day, but almost never all day long. And it was never cold. Even now, in the middle of winter, the most it got was a little chilly. The trade winds blew a lot of the time, too, and even the steady wind wasn't cold.

Janey liked the phrase—"trade winds." Back in Kansas the only names the wind had were "goldurned winds," or "dust-bucket wind"—that was Grandpa's favorite name for any wind strong enough to kick up a haze. He had lived through the Dust Bowl; he told stories about dust storms that made Janey shiver.

"I like the wind here," she said aloud. It was true. The wind on Oahu was never fierce or freezing, and it didn't raise a wall of dust. It whistled and sang its way down the mountainsides.

"Janey?" Michael interrupted her thoughts.

Janey looked at him and smiled, noticing for the first time that his hair was sticking up on one side. Mom would have to wet it to plaster it down. Michael had hair like Dad's—it did what it wanted to do.

"Janey!" he repeated, and this time he scuffed one foot on the floor as he spoke.

"Don't stamp your feet," she said, imitating her mother's voice without meaning to.

"I smell Mom's coffee," Michael said suddenly.

Janey turned and realized he was right. That meant

breakfast would be coming before too much longer. "Pancakes?" she whispered.

Michael grinned. "I hope so." Janey took his hand, and they started out the door, but a sharp slamming sound made Janey turn back. It had come from across the street and it had sounded like Mrs. Fujiwara's front door closing—hard.

"What was that?" Michael whispered.

Janey shook her head. "Maybe Mrs. Fujiwara's doing chores outside or something."

Michael frowned, listening. "Maybe . . ." He sounded worried, and Janey knew he was wondering if Mrs. Fujiwara had heard him shouting and was upset.

Janey tousled his hair. "I bet I know where some tangerines are."

Michael's face lit up. He released her hand and danced down the hallway toward the kitchen. Janey was right behind him, trying to cheer herself up. Maybe they wouldn't stay in Hawaii much longer. Maybe they could go back to Kansas, where the weather got cold and people were plain and familiar and she could have friends and not feel left out of everything all the time. Janey glanced back out her window and saw a shooting star. She closed her eyes to make a wish. "I just want to go home," she whispered.

Michael half turned. "What?"

She smiled and shrugged and followed him into the kitchen.

CHAPTER TWO

The overhead light in the kitchen seemed too glaring, the way it did every morning. The bright yellow walls seemed too yellow, too. Their house back in Kansas had had blue walls, a quiet color like the sky.

Mom was at the counter, stirring a bowl of creamy batter.

"Pancakes?" Michael breathed, sounding like he did in church when he knew he had to keep quiet.

Mom smiled. "Pancakes, and tangerines from our very own tree! What a grand morning this is."

Janey nodded. Her mother got so excited about the tangerines, it was funny. But they *were* delicious, and there was something magical about picking the bright orange fruit just steps from the back door. For the tenth time, Janey promised herself she would write Tilly a letter soon. Then she wished, for the hundredth time, that Tilly was a better letter writer. It was hard to keep writing when there were so few replies.

"I was talking to Mrs. Engers yesterday," Mom was

saying. "She says we can grow almost anything here. We'll plant a garden like no one in Kansas ever dreamed about!" She slid the spatula beneath a pancake and flipped it neatly. She opened the oven. There was a plate already stacked with the steaming pancakes. Janey's mouth watered. Mom was the world's best pancake maker.

"We won't need to go into Honolulu to the Piggly Wiggly as often once I have a good garden," Mom said.

Janey nodded, but her heart sank a little. She loved going into Honolulu to the grocery store. She heard more languages in the Piggly Wiggly grocery store here than she had heard in Topeka, Kansas, during her whole life!

"We'll grow lettuce and corn and tomatoes and everything else we used to grow back home," Mom went on, still smiling. She looked especially pretty in the morning, Janey thought. She had dark hair and eyebrows—she always looked like she had on makeup when she almost never did.

"I want to plant a cherimoya tree," Janey said.

"That green fruit Miss Watanabe sends home?" Mom asked. "With the pattern like alligator skin?"

Janey nodded. There was nothing like the juicy, delicious cherimoyas in Kansas, that much was certain. Nothing even close.

Her mother was smiling. "Lettuce won't take more than a few weeks here, I bet. It's so warm at night, even in the middle of winter!"

Janey didn't say anything. Her mother sounded enthusiastic, *too* enthusiastic. Were her parents really planning to stay in Hawaii? How could they do that? How could they just decide without even asking her? Janey took a breath, about to confront her mother, but she didn't want to admit she had listened outside the kitchen door when they hadn't known she was there. Outside, Pokey let loose one more sharp bark. Then another.

"What is that dog barking at now?" Mom asked, leaning to look out the kitchen window.

Janey crossed to the window and looked out. The stars were invisible now, and the horizon was lightening a little; dawn wasn't far off. There was a silhouette on the top rail of the yard fence, and Janey squinted, trying to see more clearly. As she stared, the indistinct shape straightened and arched its back. Pokey barked louder, bounding in a stiff-legged circle, then facing the fence again.

"It's a cat," Janey said.

"Go see if you can run it off," Mom said from the stove. She lifted another pancake from the pan and transferred it to the plate in the oven. The scent of the steam made Janey's mouth water again.

"Janey?" Mom prompted. "Go try to shoo it home, then come straight back inside. Breakfast is nearly ready."

As Janey went down the steps, the sweet perfume

of the Hawaiian night drifted around her. At home in Topeka, it was probably snowing. Here, it was so warm that she didn't even really need her sweater. The air felt soft against her face. A tiny breeze rattled the dark leaves of the tangerine tree.

"Pokey?" Janey called. The barking stopped instantly. The little terrier came bounding toward her, panting. "Pokey, you need to lose weight," Janey teased her. She *was* a chubby little dog, her body shaped like a sausage. Mom fed her too many scraps.

Janey glanced at the fence. The cat was still there, lying motionless as though it were a part of the railing. It was smart, that was obvious. It was well out of Pokey's jumping range.

Pokey faced the cat and barked twice, quick short yaps that rang out in the silence. Janey looked across the street. Mrs. Fujiwara's roosters made more noise than Pokey ever would, but that wouldn't matter if the dog had awakened the stern woman across the street. Janey couldn't see a light on. Maybe they had gotten lucky.

"You have to hush!" Janey commanded. Pokey ran back to circle her ankles, panting loudly. Janey waved her arms at the cat. It stood, startled, then delicately leaped to the ground, disappearing into the dawn-dust so quickly, she wasn't quite sure which way it had run. Neither was Pokey. The little dog bounded forward, then stopped, tilting her head and whimpering. Janey pressed her hand against her lips to keep from laughing.

"Breakfast is ready," Mom called from the back door.

Janey patted her leg, and Pokey turned toward the sound. "Come on, Pokey. Let's go in now."

"Pancakes, Jaaaaaaaney . . . ," Michael squealed from the back door, trailing out her name like a high-pitched train whistle. Janey heard her mother shushing him. Janey glanced across the street as she started for the door. The Fujiwara house was still dark, but that didn't mean anything. The front window was their living room. Their kitchen was at the back of the house.

The kitchen light seemed too bright all over again when Janey came inside. Pokey clicked across the linoleum to stand looking up at the stove.

"Not now," Mom scolded her. "How can you beg right after you do your best to wake up our neighbors?"

"Pokey loves pancakes!" Michael shouted, loud and giggly again.

Mom turned, gesturing with the spatula. "Young man, lower your voice. It's too early to shout like that. Sit down and mind your manners." She glanced at Janey. "Was it a cat?"

Janey nodded. "It took off. Mrs. Fujiwara's house still looks dark."

"Oh, she's up, I imagine," Mom said, echoing Janey's

thoughts. "You know how early they go to work in their taro patch. I wonder about them, and I keep thinking I should go over and chat, but she just isn't very—"

"Friendly," Janey finished for her mother as she pulled out the chair across from Michael.

"It's a shame," Mom said, carrying over two plates. There was a dish of tangerines sitting in the center of the table. Janey reached out to touch one. It was cold. Mom put them in the fridge to chill. Mom had heated the syrup, and the butter was soft. Janey ate her pancakes slowly, feeling almost normal, as though her life hadn't been turned upside down in Kansas then shaken out here—onto a speck of land in the middle of the Pacific Ocean.

Janey stood beside her mother at the sink, rinsing and drying the dishes. Outside, the sun was glimmering on the horizon. Mom turned on the radio, resting her hands on the top of the polished maple cabinet as it crackled and hissed, waiting for the tubes to warm up.

Janey plopped into a chair, and Michael frowned. He didn't like the radio; it meant he had to be quiet.

"This is KGMB, Hawaii," the announcer said. "With music for your listening pleasure this fine Sunday morning, December seventh, nineteen forty-one." Then a soft song began. Janey loved music, especially the big bands. Closing her eyes, she let the beautiful sounds wash over her.

"Has Daddy given you a dancing lesson lately?" Mom asked.

Janey opened her eyes and smiled. "No."

Mom shook her head. "Well, we need to remind him. Pretty girls who can dance, too"—she arched her brows—"girls like that can always get dates."

Janey blushed. Her mother seemed sure that, when Janey was older, boys would think she was pretty. She wasn't nearly as sure. She knew she was too tall, for one thing, and far too skinny. "I like dancing," she said aloud, because her mother was looking at her, waiting for some kind of response.

"Well, of course you do," Mom teased. "You are your father's daughter. And mine." She made a cartoonish frowning face. She looked like Blondie in the funny papers when she was mad at Dagwood for something.

Janey grinned at her own thoughts.

"What's so funny?" her mother asked.

"Nothing," Janey answered, tapping her feet. "I do love music."

"You'll be a good driver, too, like your mother." Mom smiled. She was proud of being a better driver than Dad—than most any man. She had grown up in Kansas driving hay trucks and tractors and harvest equipment from when she was eight years old. Grandpa had strapped blocks of wood to the pedals so she could reach them.

"I hope so," Janey said, then they both fell silent, listening to the swinging rhythm of the band.

Mom reached out and turned the big brass-colored knob to raise the volume. Janey loved to watch her parents dance. At her cousin Shirley's wedding the year before, they had stopped the whole reception, and people had applauded when the song ended. Janey looked at her pretty mother and wondered if she would ever be half as beautiful. Probably not, she thought, then she whispered what Grandma always said whenever she worried about this kind of stuff out loud: "Pretty is as pretty does."

Michael suddenly flopped sideways on the divan, sighing to let them know he was bored.

"Do you want to learn to dance?" Mom asked him.

Michael shook his head, frowning.

"Are you sure?" Janey asked. She wanted her mother to get up and dance, because she wanted to watch. Her mother would be good at the hula, she was pretty sure. Mom was naturally graceful.

Michael was shaking his head, wearing the stubborn look that let everyone know there was no point in arguing with him. "I am too little to dance," he said solemnly. He sat up slowly, glaring at the radio.

"No one is ever too little," Mom said evenly.

"I am too little," Michael insisted. "Shirley stepped on my foot and nearly broke it." He lifted a foot to look at it as though it had been permanently damaged.

"At the wedding?" Janey asked him. He nodded, and she tried not to laugh at how serious he looked.

"That was probably her fault," Mom said, "and I'm sure she was very sorry."

Michael nodded somberly. "She said she was. But she danced fine with Ralph. He's a lot bigger."

Janey exchanged a glance with her mother. Ralph was Shirley's new husband.

"You might be right," Janey told her brother, even though Mom arched her brows. "He *is* pretty little to dance," Janey said, facing her mother. Her brows went up ever farther. Janey sighed. Her mother had the idea that people could do whatever they wanted to do—whatever they set their minds to. Janey thought this might be true some of the time—but sometimes it wasn't. Tilly O'Neill was so shy that she threw up when she had to give a book report in front of the class. She was sick the whole day before she had to recite a tiny part in a skit in fourth grade. Mom just kept saying Tilly should set her mind to it and not worry so much. Tilly tried. But she still threw up.

"What are you thinking?" Janey's mother asked her.

"I was thinking about Tilly," Janey said quietly.

"I know you miss her, honey," her mother said, her voice soft and sympathetic. "I miss everyone, too."

Janey looked into her mother's face and realized she hadn't thought much about her mother being lonely. The truth was, Mom made friends everywhere—and she made them easily. She already belonged to a bridge club that got together to play cards once a week, and she had been asked to help out at the school Christmas party.

Janey wasn't like that. She barely talked to anyone outside Miss Watanabe's music room where the other girls all chatted with their friends—and she really didn't talk too much anywhere else at school either.

"Look what a beautiful day it's going to be," Janey's mother said abruptly, changing the subject as she often did when something upset her. She smiled. "I hope your father gets back in time to catch lots of fish for our supper tonight." She came back to sit down beside Michael, tickling him until he stopped looking grumpy.

The program on the radio changed. The First Baptist Church of Waikiki began the introduction to their Sunday broadcast service. For a while, they all sat in silence, Janey and her mother listening while Michael squirmed and fidgeted between them. He got up and began to play on the floor. He pulled off one shoe and pushed it along, making sounds like a car.

Janey closed her eyes for a moment, then opened them abruptly.

"Is something wrong?" her mother asked.

Janey stared out the window. The long leaves of the banana trees were fluttering in the breeze. The sun was streaming down the mountain slopes now, bright and warm. Janey closed her eyes again. There was a steady thrumming sound in the distance. She opened the window and listened.

"Janey?" her mother asked. "Do you see something out there? Is Mrs. Fujiwara coming?"

Janey shook her head, and Michael bounced off the divan to come look outside. "It's planes," he said.

Janey nodded. "Are there China Clippers coming in from the mainland today?"

Mom shrugged. "I don't know."

"Do they ever do military maneuvers on Sundays?" Janey wondered aloud, trying to remember. There were several military airfields on Oahu, and all the pilots had to train in their warplanes. "It could be the navy having a drill," Janey said, hoping she was wrong, as the sound got louder. The China Clippers would just land on their huge pontoons in Pearl Harbor and unload the tourists coming from the States. A military drill would mean hours of ear-shattering noise. She hated it. They were practicing in case there was a war, she knew. The drills made her think about the war in Europe, and she didn't want to think about it.

"Look," Mom said from just behind her. She leaned forward to point.

Janey saw Mrs. Fujiwara was standing out in her yard, peering into the east and shading her eyes. "She hears the planes, too," Janey said.

The words had barely left her mouth when she heard a faint booming sound. Her mother gasped, a constricted little sound that scared Janey more than anything else. "What's wrong?" she asked.

Janey's mother smiled tightly. "Nothing. Just all the war talk lately. That sound startled me, that's all. I'm tired of these battle drills. To be honest, the noise gets hard to bear."

"Me, too," Janey agreed, nodding. Michael imitated her, his face solemn.

"It just startled me," Mom repeated. "But I'm sure it's just another drill."

Janey watched. In the morning sun, rows of silvery planes were coming in—and flying so low that Janey could clearly see the orange circles painted on their sides. For a moment she didn't allow herself to realize the truth. *The navy painted these planes for the drill,* she heard herself thinking. That's all it was—just a drill like all the rest.

But as the planes came closer, Janey knew that wasn't true. They were so low, she could see the pilots, sitting rigid and staring straight ahead. These were Japanese soldiers, Japanese pilots. And they were attacking. The ground shook with the force of bombs exploding.

CHAPTER THREE

Michael burst out crying, and Janey's mother picked him up. A second explosion vibrated through the house, shaking the windows.

"Get away from the glass!" Mom yelled.

Janey turned to look at her mother. Michael had pressed his face into her hair, his hands knotted together around her neck. Janey watched as Mom picked up the phone, then set the receiver back in its cradle. Then she whirled and crossed the room to turn the radio up higher. A recorded choir was singing now, a magnificent arrangement of a hymn Janey didn't recognize.

Another explosion shook the house. Janey stepped back from the window, remembering what her mother had shouted at her minutes before. Or had it been seconds?

Yet another blast shook the walls, and Michael screamed. Janey's mother suddenly turned on her heel and ran for the back door. "Janey, come on!" she shouted back over her shoulder.

Janey wasn't conscious of following her mother, but somehow she ended up out on the lawn, the back door standing wide open. She looked up, shading her eyes from the early morning sunshine. The droning roar of the planes seemed to fill the world. It was impossible to tell which direction any of the sounds were coming from—they just seemed to saturate the very air.

A series of explosions rocked the ground beneath their feet. "Maybe we should get back inside!" Janey's mother shouted. She gestured wildly. "Go back in!"

"Back inside?" Janey whirled around, but her mother only stared without saying anything else. Another explosion shuddered through the soil.

Where should they run? Was inside safer than outside? What if the house collapsed? Janey felt trapped, even though she was standing in the open. Her heartbeat seemed ragged, and she was breathing hard, as though she had been running. Michael had gone still in Mom's arms. He clung to her, hiding his face in her hair. Janey glanced toward the harbor. Black clouds of roiling smoke were rising. It took her a moment to realize what could possibly be burning on the water. The battleships—the huge floating cities full of sailors and officers—were being hit.

A movement caught Janey's eye, and she realized Mrs. Fujiwara was running toward them. She yelled something as she got closer, but her voice was lost in the roar of the planes. Her face was contorted, as though the words hurt as they came from her mouth. Janey stared at Mrs. Fujiwara, trying to understand what she was saying. But just as she reached the banana trees at the edge of their yard, she veered off, running down the road.

The force of another explosion quivered through the ground, and Janey stared as Mrs. Fujiwara kept going, running awkwardly, her heavy dark dress flapping out. She was usually so dignified, so calm—it was strange to see her so obviously frightened. A plane flew over so low that they all bent double, ducking instinctively, Mrs. Fujiwara first, then Janey, then her mother. Janey straightened to see her mother lying sprawled sideways on the grass. Michael lay beside her, crying hard.

"Are you all right?" Janey screamed, running toward them. "Mom?"

"Janey?" Mom was turning sideways, trying to sit up with Michael still wrapped around her. He was wriggling now.

"Are you all right?" Janey could feel her kneecaps jumping; it was as though her whole body wanted to run, to get away from the thrumming of the plane engines overhead and the sound of the bombs going off in the harbor.

"I was running and I just . . . tripped," Mom said, sitting up slowly. Her eyes looked empty, stunned. Janey glanced upward. The planes were out over the harbor now. Would they come back and drop bombs here? Mom was glancing up at the sky, then toward the harbor, standing up slowly. "Your father . . . ," she began.

Janey's heart skipped a beat. "Do you think they attacked Hickam Field?"

Michael twisted out of her mother's arms and slid to the ground. Mom bent over to keep one hand clasped around his arm. "We need to get away from the harbor," she said in a shaky voice.

Janey's knees shook, and she shivered as if they were standing in a snowstorm, not in the sunshine of a warm Hawaiian morning. "We should wait here for Daddy," she said so softly that she knew her mother couldn't possibly have heard her, so she cleared her throat and repeated it. "We should stay here. Daddy will come looking for us any minute."

Mom nodded slowly, frowning. "Then we can all get away from the military bases."

"Would the Japanese pilots bomb Honolulu?" Janey asked.

A look of tortured uncertainty crossed her mother's face. "I don't know."

Janey felt a prickling of fear creep into her heart. There were thousands of people in Honolulu. Then the fear she dreaded most took over her thoughts. Daddy. Was her father all right?

Janey glanced down the road. Maybe a military jeep would come roaring up the road any second. Her father would wait until the driver was almost stopped, then he would vault out of the seat and run to hug them all. He would be fine. He would be smiling. And he would take care of them. He would know what to do.

"We can't leave!" Janey yelled at her mother as another plane droned past, flying a little higher than the first wave, but not much, sweeping on a long, descending path toward the battleships in Pearl Harbor. Janey saw her mother look skyward. "What if Daddy comes back?"

Mom nodded, and Janey saw how confused and desperate she was, how scared. Planes were coming over again, and these were so low that they seemed impossibly huge. Janey felt her knees buckling in an irresistible urge to get down, lie flat, *disappear*.

"Inside!" Janey's mother screamed. "Back in the house!"

She turned to pick up Michael and then froze. Janey glanced around, turning in a slow, panicky circle, trying to spot her brother.

"Janey! Get inside!" Mom was shrieking now, gesturing furiously.

Janey started for the door, then hesitated. Her mother grabbed her arm, pinching hard. "Michael probably ran back inside," she shouted into Janey's ear. "If he's there, signal me from the door." Mom was staring into her eyes. "Don't come back out, do you hear me?"

Janey nodded as her mother spun around, running toward the banana trees. But instead of heading for the house, Janey stood still, watching her mother dash across the lawn. Of course, Janey thought. Michael often played among the thick, slanted banana trunks. Unable to stand still a second longer, Janey sprinted to catch up, then ignored her mother's glare and ran beside her. She was scared of the planes and the bombs and she was scared for her brother. Most of all, she was scared to be alone while the planes were droning overhead.

More explosions erupted out over the harbor, and a single plane flew above them, a little higher. An odd staccato whistling made Janey look up. An uneven line of planes was approaching. The strange whistling sound got louder, then changed to a violent rattling, then was drowned out in the sound of the engines. It wasn't until Janey saw tufts of grass being kicked up across the lawn that she realized what was happening. The planes were shooting! Maybe they meant to hit the battleships in the harbor, but their bullets were ripping downward and hitting here, right here! Janey screamed without meaning to, and her legs trembled. Her body wanted to run, was desperate to run, but everywhere she looked, the little spurts of grass and dirt told her bullets were raining down.

"Get inside!" Mom shrieked, but Janey set her feet wider and clutched at her mother's arm, forcing her into holding still until the planes had passed over-head and the last of the bullets had buried themselves deep in the dirt.

"We have to find Michael!" Janey shouted once the strafing had stopped. "Now! Before they come again!" Then she sprinted for the house, shouting Michael's name. Behind her, she heard her mother calling him just as frantically.

Breathing hard, she felt a stinging in her throat and realized that a haze of smoke was drifting in from the harbor as she leaped up the steps and pounded into the kitchen. She tore through the house toward Michael's bedroom.

"Michael?" She dropped to her knees to look under the bed.

"Michael?" He wasn't there. She scrambled up again. She could hear her mother still shouting Michael's name outside. The sounds of the explosions were more distant now, but the planes could come back at any second.

Still breathing hard, Janey eyed the old wardrobe against the wall. She crossed the room and flung open the doors. Michael's clothes and his toys were inside, messy as usual. But Michael was nowhere to be seen.

"Please answer me!" Janey yelled. "Michael, come on!" But there was no response.

She ran to her own room, then her parents', then double-checked every hiding place she could think of.

Her mother's voice was getting ragged and strained, but the calling kept up, first in front of the house, then in back.

Suddenly Janey noticed the radio was still on. She turned it up and heard an angelic chorus of voices singing. *"All is well, all is well."* Then the music cut off abruptly, and a man began to talk. He identified himself as the governor, Joseph Poindexter. His voice was shaking. Janey blinked back tears, listening, as he confirmed her worst fears.

This was a real attack. It was war. The planes were Japanese planes, not painted-up drill-dummies . . . and the bombs and strafing bullets were no mistake; they were real and would kill. Governor Poindexter cleared his throat. "This is no drill," he emphasized. "This is the real McCoy."

Then the church music came back on. Janey could hear scraping noises in the background as though someone at the radio station was moving furniture around. What was going on? Janey whirled to run for the door.

The roaring sounds of bombs and planes slammed against her ears and jolted her heart as she went outside and stumbled to a stop, looking upward. She hesitated in the door frame, afraid to step into the open. Then she heard her mother's voice.

"Janey? Janey!" Mom shouted hoarsely. "I found him! I've got Michael!"

Janey leaped from the top step to the grass. Suddenly nothing was more important in the world than seeing her little brother, knowing that he was all right. She rounded the corner of the house and nearly ran into her mother. Michael was back in her arms like an oversized toddler, his face buried in her hair again.

"Where was he?" Janey asked.

Mom glanced back over her shoulder. "Behind the garden shed. All balled up and crying." She glared at the sky, her face contorted as though she was about to start crying herself.

"Where's Pokey?" Janey asked suddenly, ashamed that she hadn't thought about the little terrier before this.

Mom frowned. "I don't know. I'll find her if I can."

"We have to find her," Janey said, tears stinging at their eyes.

"I'll look," Mom said, her voice steadier now. "You get in the car with Michael," she ordered Janey. "And you stay put and wait for me. I'm going to leave your father a note." She slid Michael downward, gently loosening his hands from around her neck. "Janey will take care of you, honey. Go get in the car."

"Bring Pokey when you come back, Mom," Janey said.

"I'll try. But we have to get out of here, Janey," her mother said without looking back as Janey reached down to take Michael's hand.

Michael didn't want to come with Janey. She had to pull him along, trying to reassure him and keep him moving at the same time. It wasn't easy. He dragged his feet and nearly sat down twice, acting like he had when he was two years old. Janey glanced back. Mom was disappearing into the house.

The instant Janey let go of Michael's hand to open the heavy front door of the Buick, he sat down in the dirt, glaring up at her. "I don't want to go, Janey."

She tried to smile at him so that he wouldn't be as afraid, and kept one eye on him as she grabbed the door handle. She pushed the door wide, turning to prop it open with her hip as she reached for Michael's hand. "Let's get in, Michael," she said in the calmest voice she could manage. Her hands were trembling a little and her kneecaps still felt twitchy.

"Where's Daddy?" Michael asked suddenly, and Janey pulled in a quick breath.

"He should be here soon," she said. "He was going to go fishing with Mr. Wilkins, remember? Mom is leaving him a note in case we miss him, though."

Janey was at a loss for any more to say. She was terrified for her father and she was afraid her own fear would leak into her voice if she tried to speak another word.

"Okay," Michael said. He seemed to accept her explanation and stepped upward, reaching for the edge of the seat. Janey boosted him from behind, and he tumbled in, lying down. As he scooted over without sitting up, Janey climbed in after him and closed the door—but not hard enough. Feeling unsteady, she shoved the handle down, opened the door, and slammed it tight the second time.

"Come on, Michael," she pleaded. "You have to sit up. How can Mom drive if there's no place for her to sit?"

Michael rolled over on the wide seat, lying facedown. Janey could see his shoulders shaking and she knew that he was crying. She felt tears in her own eyes and turned to look once more toward the harbor. There was a wall of billowing black smoke now that hid the wetlands and the harbor. Janey scrunched down in the seat so she could look up at the empty blue sky. The planes would come back, wouldn't they? If not now, they would come back tomorrow or the next day. With more bombs and more bullets. This was war. The war she had gotten so tired of hearing about—the war her father thought would never come to Hawaii. It was here. It was here, and her father was very likely somewhere in the middle of the bombing.

"When will Daddy be back?" Michael asked.

"Soon, I hope," Janey told him, unable to lie around the painful tightness in her throat.

CHAPTER FOUR

The sunshine was turning an eerie color, filtered by the oily smoke. In the strange orangish light, Janey lay sideways, curled up around her little brother, holding him close. Then, after a few minutes, she managed to sit up, pulling him with her.

The way the Buick was parked, Janey could see the house across the road. Mrs. Fujiwara's shed was on fire. Her stomach tightening, Janey twisted around in the seat so she could see some of the houses farther up the road. There was a trickle of smoke coming from the roof of one house. Janey could see people running back and forth, but they were too far away for her to tell what they were doing.

Staring, Janey saw another, larger fire starting in an outbuilding behind the house. It was growing fast, fed by a stack of fruit crates leaning against the wall. Were all the houses going to burn down?

The sound of an engine startled Janey, and she saw a black sedan go past, the driver hunched forward over the steering wheel. At the corner, the car turned sharply left, heading toward the government road.

"The radio isn't playing anything but music," Mom said as she opened the driver's door. "I thought maybe someone would tell us what this was all about and—"

"It was a real attack," Janey said quickly, and explained what she'd heard.

Her mother slumped against the seat. "I wish I knew where to go. Or if we should just wait here for your father and—"

"Where's Pokey?" Michael asked.

Mom sighed, looking at him, then at Janey. "I couldn't find her. She's not under the beds. I looked everywhere. She must have run off."

"We can't leave her behind," Janey said, shaking her head. She could feel tears pressing behind her eyes, making them sting. "I don't want to leave," she managed to say. "I want to wait for Daddy." Her voice sounded shaky and whiny, and she pulled in a breath to settle down, but couldn't.

"Listen," Mom said, holding her finger to her lips. Janey heard the distant rumbling; it was the sound of plane engines. Janey felt Michael tense.

Abruptly, making a little sound deep in her throat, Janey's mother turned the key, slamming the car into gear. She backed up fast, then cranked the wheel and the tires skidded a little, the car sliding in a half circle. Mom put out her right arm, stiff and straight, to make sure they didn't end up on the floor. She always did that when she had to turn or brake hard.

The Buick raised a cloud of dust as the back tires slewed around. Janey stared up at her mother's profile—her eyes were intent, her jaw set. Mom steered hard to the left and the car straightened, then she peered straight ahead, both hands gripping the wheel so hard that her knuckles were white.

"What about The Fujiwaras?" Janey said. "They don't have a car."

Her mother didn't answer, but she braked, her right arm swinging out again to brace Janey and Michael. She gestured at the Fujiwaras' house. "Run, Janey. I didn't see if Mrs. Fujiwara came back. But check if anyone is there and if they want to come with us."

Janey looked out the window at the Fujiwaras' house. The shed fire was burning brighter, the flames crawling over the unpainted wood planks. Nodding, Janey leaned down on the door handle and heard the steel catch release.

"If I honk, it means more planes are coming," her Mother said evenly. "If you hear the horn, just get back here quick."

"I will," Janey promised, getting out. But her knees felt shaky again, and she didn't want to move away from the car. The door handle felt cold beneath her fingers.

"Run!" her mother repeated.

Janey pushed herself off the side of the car and jumped over the shallow ditch that drained the road. She sprinted to the Fujiwaras' front door. She stopped, breathless, and knocked. It sounded absurdly soft after the plane's roar and the booming of the bombs. She knocked again, much harder.

"Come on, Mrs. Fujiwara," Janey whispered, shifting her weight from one foot to the other. "Just open the door if you're back. *Come on!*"

The unnerving stillness continued. Janey couldn't hear a sound from inside the house. The only sound outside came from the idling car engine and the distant thump and shudder of bombs. *"Please,"* Janey hissed at the closed door. And, as though it had somehow heard her, it opened a crack.

Janey leaned forward. "I'm Janey from across the road and I—"

"I know who you are," a voice said. "I am Akiko." The door eased a few more inches back, and a girl's face appeared. She was pretty and pale and she looked as scared as Janey felt. "I hope no one in your family is hurt."

"We're fine," Janey said. "My father isn't here, though. He had to work at Hickam Field this morning."

Janey saw a shadow of sadness pass through Akiko's eyes, and she lifted one hand to stop whatever Akiko was thinking. "He's all right, though."

Janey heard how hollow and worried her voice sounded and she didn't care. Her father *was* all right. He had to be. "Is your mother here? Do you want to go with us?"

Akiko shook her head. "My mother went to find my father. I am to stay here and wait for them." Then she pulled in a quick breath. "But I would appreciate a ride to the taro field."

Janey nodded. "Sure. My mother won't mind. I wanted to come meet you before," she said, glancing up long enough to meet Akiko's eyes, then looking away when Akiko looked aside without speaking. The silence went on for a few seconds, and Janey had no idea what to say. "Let's go," she said finally. Akiko hesitated, then opened the door wide enough to step through the opening and stand on the porch. Janey took a step back. "I'm pretty scared," Janey said, without knowing she was going to say it.

Akiko didn't answer. She glanced back through the door.

"My mother left my father a note," Janey said.

Akiko turned and disappeared inside, leaving the door open. In seconds she reappeared, carrying a cloth bag. "The taro field is not too far. It's—"

"We see you working there sometimes," Janey said quickly. *But no one in your family ever waves or even looks up,* she thought, but didn't say. It figured that Akiko would be as unfriendly as her mother. They stood a few more awkward seconds in silence, then the Buick horn bleated.

Janey whirled around to face the road. "That means my mother hears planes coming."

Akiko's face paled. She started back inside, then stopped when Janey grabbed her hand. "Come with us. Did you write a note for your mother?"

Akiko nodded. "In case I missed her, but—"

"Then let's go," Janey insisted. The sound of the plane engines grated at her nerves. "Hurry!"

Akiko nodded again and closed the door behind her. Janey led the way toward the car, running as fast as she could in her skirt and wishing she had worn slacks.

Janey opened the back door for Akiko and waited while she clambered up into the high seat. Then she slammed the door shut and scrambled into the front seat beside her brother.

"Where's Mrs. Fujiwara?" Janey's mother demanded. "Is this all right with her?"

Janey shrugged. "I think so. Akiko just wants a ride to their taro field. That's where her mother went—she wanted to find Akiko's father. She was supposed to come right back, but . . ." Janey trailed off and watched her mother's face darken.

The planes were getting closer. Janey watched her mother slide the gearshift upward. Then, without saying another word, she began to drive.

They were a good mile down the road when the Buick slowed and Janey sat upright to see better. "Look at that," Mom whispered.

Janey stretched up to see out the windshield. There, ahead of them and coming fast, was a line of military vehicles. Most of them were crammed with passengers. Men were shirtless, trying to get dressed. One man was pulling trousers on over his pajamas, standing up in the back of a truck. A few were hanging half out of the trucks. The two jeeps in front were using both lanes.

"How can we possibly . . . ?" Mom began angrily, then she braked, hard. There was no choice. The road was narrow, and there was nowhere to turn off. She shouted for them to hang on and her arm shot out. Janey braced her feet against the floor and held Michael steady as the car skidded to a stop. She heard Akiko's gasp of surprise and felt her thump into the back of the front seat.

Janey watched, stunned, as the jeep on their side of the road slammed to a stop as well, and a soldier leaped out and ran toward them.

CHAPTER FIVE

"Get your car off the road, ma'am," the soldier ordered tersely, approaching the driver's side of the Buick.

"My husband is down at Hickam Field—" Janey's mother began, but the soldier cut her off.

"What rank?"

"Civilian," Mom answered. "He's a welding expert they brought in from Kansas. Have you heard anything about the airfields? I . . ." Janey's mother trailed off. The soldier wasn't even looking at her. Janey stared at the man. He looked tense enough to explode as he watched the vehicles in the other lane stream past.

"Civilian? I can't do anything for you, then, ma'am," he said suddenly. He slapped the car roof, and Janey cringed at the sudden sound. "Get this car off the road."

"There's nowhere to turn off!" Janey's mother answered.

The soldier scowled, jabbing an angry index finger

at the air, indicating the grassy field the road bordered.

"Get out of the way, ma'am," he shouted. "Clear the road!" Then he bent down and peered into the window, shifting so that he was looking into the backseat. "Where'd you get the little Jap girl?"

Janey glanced backward and saw Akiko's face stiffen, then set into a rigid expression of disinterest.

"She's my neighbor's daughter," Mom was saying tersely. "Her mother was gone when we were ready to leave, and I—"

"Gone where?" the soldier pressed.

Mom licked her lips, clearly nervous. As she hesitated, Michael began to squirm.

"Her mother had gone to find her father," Janey said as loud as she could. Then she stretched up to see over the backseat again. "That's right, isn't it, Akiko?"

Akiko nodded.

"I thought it was safer for her to come with us and to get away from the harbor," Mom said.

The soldier straightened, his hand resting lightly on the car fender. "Safer for who?" he asked in a tight voice, then scowled at Akiko.

Janey hated him for an instant. They were all scared enough, upset enough . . . didn't he have something more important to do than frighten and insult a girl?

"Sir, there's no reason to—" Mom began.

"Get the car off the road, ma'am," he shouted.

Janey's mother shoved the gearshift downward and threw the car in reverse. She backed up about twenty feet, then pulled the car forward, turning the wheel hard, hand over hand, to veer off the road and into the field beside it, swinging wide to miss a Christmas berry bush that sprawled low along the ground. Janey liked the bushes—they were pretty. She stared at this one as her mother maneuvered the car in angry little hitches and jerks. The bush was studded with vivid red berries and droppings from the birds that came to eat them.

The instant the Buick was out of the way, the jeep in their lane started forward again. Janey could hear the men shouting to each other, calling back and forth in the vehicles as they passed, asking about friends, trying to find out who had been aboard what ship.

Janey turned to look at the cloud bank of oily smoke rising from the harbor. Some of the sailors stayed onshore while others lived onboard the ships. The men were trying to find out who might be hurt and who was safe. She thought about her father and for an instant imagined him lying hurt. Then she squeezed her eyes shut and reopened them, willing the thought away. Daddy was fine. He had to be fine.

Janey's mother put the car in gear once the long line of vehicles had passed. She eased back onto the road and drove on, going more slowly. "Roll down the windows," she said.

Janey glanced back to see Akiko obeying. Her own

window crank was stiff, and it took Janey a full minute or more to work it downward.

"Now help me listen," Mom said. "For planes, more trucks, anything unusual. Where's the taro field exactly, Akiko?" she added, glancing backward.

"Not far, ma'am," Akiko answered.

"On the right, yes?" Janey asked.

Akiko nodded, then sat back to stare out her window.

Janey turned and faced front again. Michael was fidgeting as he always did in the car. Usually she played some silly guessing game with him. Today she couldn't seem to think of anything. They drove through the middle of town. It was weirdly empty and silent. Janey eyed the Pearl City Theater as they passed. The metal roof looked undamaged. Next to it, the signs in the windows of Esther's Diner made her feel strange. Cherry Coke seemed like something wonderful from another planet—one with quiet skies and no billows of black smoke snaking skyward. She turned to look back toward the harbor. There was nothing to see but that awful wall of smoke.

"Which way?" Mom asked suddenly, turning to glance at Akiko in the backseat.

"Turn left past the store. Then just drive alongside the train tracks for a ways."

Janey's mother followed Akiko's directions, and Janey looked out to watch the green fields skim past. Michael slumped against her as though he were sleepy—except that his eyes were wide open, and he was leaning forward a little. After a moment, Janey realized why: He was staring out through the windshield. He was keeping watch on the sky.

A few minutes later, Akiko made a small sound in the backseat, and Janey knew her mother had heard it because the car slowed. "Here?" Mom asked.

Janey stretched up and turned to see over the back of the seat. Akiko was on her knees, leaning out the window.

"Here?" Mom repeated.

"Yes," Akiko said in a low voice.

Mom braked to a gentle stop.

Akiko shoved down on the door handle and got out, then stood uncertainly.

"Where are they?" Janey asked. The taro was lush and green, but not that tall. The field was perfectly flat. There was nothing to hide anyone from sight. Akiko's parents were not here.

Akiko took a step away from the car, then hesitated again.

"Akiko?" Mom called.

The girl turned, and Janey could see how upset she was. "Perhaps I should walk back to my house," Akiko said.

"I can't leave you here alone," Mom said sternly.

Akiko flushed and looked at her shoes. "I am so sorry to have taken you out of your way, ma'am.

I should never have disobeyed my mother."

"I will take you home if that's what you want," Mom said.

Akiko bit at her lower lip, then nodded. She got into the backseat. Janey's mother shifted into reverse, looking behind them at a wide apron of level ground on one side of the road.

A sudden roar of engines startled Janey as four or five planes popped out from behind the long mountain slopes that lay inland. Janey's mother braked and put the car into first gear, holding the clutch in as she turned toward the backseat. "I can't take you back there, Akiko. I can't leave you alone, either. So please come with us."

"I cannot," Akiko said flatly.

Janey saw her mother glance out at the planes. Behind them, in the harbor, was an explosion that made them all flinch.

"If your parents decided to leave the harbor, where would they go?" Mom asked.

"They would not have left me," Akiko said coldly.

"She's asking because we don't know where we should go," Janey said quietly.

"My mother planned for us to go to the cane fields," Akiko said in an unsteady voice from the backseat. "She said it would be a good place to hide, that the soldiers would not care about bombing cane."

Janey's mother nodded, then turned to glance back. "Do you know the way?"

"Yes," Akiko said. "And I will tell you. But I should stay here."

"No, you shouldn't," Mom said, easing the car forward, watching Akiko in the rearview mirror. "It isn't safe here."

Janey heard the certainty in her mother's voice and was grateful that someone was certain about something. The rest of the world seemed to be coming apart. She closed her eyes and hoped that her father was all right and that Akiko's parents were safe and that Pokey had found somewhere good to hide.

"To the right here where the pineapple fields end, then up the dirt road," Akiko said quietly.

Janey's mother half turned. "I couldn't hear you, sweetie."

Akiko cleared her throat and repeated it a little louder. Janey saw her mother nod as she slowed to make the turn, then spoke over her shoulder. "How much farther?"

When Akiko didn't answer, Janey stretched up to look over the back of the seat. Akiko's eyes were open wide, and she looked uneasy.

"She isn't sure," Janey told her mother. Akiko's face lit with a tiny smile. "But she knows the way," Janey added, and Akiko nodded.

"You just tell me which turns as we get to them, then," Mom said.

Akiko nodded. "Yes, ma'am."

Janey's mother shot her a look. "What lovely manners," she said. "I am sure your mother is proud of you."

They drove on, the sound of the planes overhead for a few minutes, then diminishing behind them. The thumping percussion of the bombs seemed distant, removed, but Janey gritted her teeth and whispered a clumsy little prayer. She saw her mother's lips moving and knew she was doing the same thing.

"Turn to the left up here, please, ma'am," Akiko said quietly. When Janey stretched up to look at her again, she pretended not to notice.

"I want to go see Daddy," Michael said suddenly.

"We will soon," Mom said, meeting Janey's eyes for a flickering instant.

"I want Pokey, too," Michael said.

"I do, too," Janey told him, trying to hug him. He squirmed free and sat with his arms crossed over his chest.

Mom glanced down at him. "Just leave him alone for a little while," she said in a half whisper. Janey nodded.

"This is the last road," Akiko said from the backseat. "Turn to the left."

Janey sat up to look around as they went on. The cane fields were broken up with fields of pineapples and bare hillsides where no one farmed the rust-colored dirt. They drove for a long time before Akiko's voice came from the backseat again. "These are my uncle's fields. He lives in Honolulu, but usually they are here working."

Mom braked, and Janey peered out. There was no house. She couldn't see anyone around, either. "Are you sure this is the right place?"

Akiko nodded. "Perhaps my uncle and aunt stayed home today. It is Sunday, and they are Catholic."

Janey's mother stretched. "Well, let's get out and look around," she said.

Janey shoved down on the door handle and climbed out, then turned to help Michael, but he slid away from her again. She opened the back door, and Akiko got out gracefully, taking care not to get too much of the reddish road dust on her shoes. Janey sighed. Akiko was the kind of girl her mother wanted *her* to be: polite and neat and clean all the time. A breeze ran through the tall cane and it hissed among the leaves.

"Oh, no," Janey heard her mother saying. "Oh, no . . . oh, no . . ."

Janey walked around the car, staring. Usually she loved to look back down on the harbor whenever they drove into the hills, but today the view was unlike anything she had ever seen—or dreamed—and her heart constricted. It looked like the world had ended below them. She shivered. Her father was somewhere in the middle of the most awful destruction she could imagine.

The heavy smoke drifted low, bellying along the

ground, then clearing with the breeze for a few seconds. The giant battleships that had been docked in majestic rows around Ford Island were in flames.

Janey heard her mother gasp and she knew why. It was impossible to see Hickam Field clearly from where they stood—the smoke was too thick. But when it parted for a second here and there, all she could see was flames. The buildings, the airplanes caught helpless on the ground—everything seemed to be on fire.

"Is that Hickam?" Mom asked in a low voice, pointing.

Janey nodded. "I think so."

"Michael?" Mom said abruptly, tearing herself away from the ugly smoke rising in the distance.

"He is here," Akiko said from the far side of the car. "I will watch him for you. I don't wish to look down there."

Janey heard the tension in Akiko's voice and she understood it perfectly. Her father, Akiko's parents, thousands more people—were they all right? How could they be? Janey swallowed hard and glanced up at her mother's profile. She was staring straight down at the harbor, and her eyes were narrowed and shiny.

The sound of plane engines startled them all. "Run into the cane," Janey's mother shouted. She shooed Janey and Akiko ahead of her, swooping Michael up to carry him.

As the throbbing roar got louder, they ducked into the rows of cane and Janey's mother ran ahead, leading the way. "It's sharp," Akiko yelled. "Don't cut yourself."

Janey felt a prickling sting on the back of one hand, and Akiko's words suddenly made sense. "The cane is sharp, Mom!" she shouted. Her mother slowed slightly but showed no other sign of hearing. Janey ran hard, trying to keep up. Akiko stayed right behind her.

Janey's mother finally slowed, then stopped, panting. Janey could still hear the planes, even over the sound of their breathing. Were they circling?

The sudden sound of bombs hitting in the distance made her spin around, but of course there was nothing to see but the dense, giant-grass leaves of the cane. Were they coming closer? Janey's mother sank to the ground and held Michael tight. Janey sat next to her, and Akiko stood a little ways away as the deep, ugly thumping sounds came closer together.

"Over here," Mom said to Akiko, and she came forward slowly, kneeling in the red dust beside Janey. "Hold hands," Mom said.

Janey took Akiko's hand, then reached for her brother's. He had his face in Mom's hair again, but when she touched him, he clasped her hand tightly.

"Do you want to pray?" Mom asked Akiko.

She nodded. "Yes."

"All right," Mom said. "Let's hold hands and pray for our families."

Janey stared at her mother. Her voice sounded too high, like a scared little girl, but her eyes were steady and calm. Janey realized suddenly that no one was holding Mom's left hand. Akiko seemed to realize it at the same instant, and she reached out to close the circle.

Janey closed her eyes and began to pray. She wasn't very good at it. Her father hated church, and they didn't go very often. But it felt like the only thing any of them could do now, and it made her feel a tiny bit better to be doing *something*.

Janey felt the breeze rise and heard the whisper of the cane all around them. She held very still, trying not to imagine what was going on down in the ugly swirling black smoke. Three or four times she opened her eyes to let the sunlit green of the cane fields chase away the dark pictures in her imagination.

The sound of the bombs came farther and farther apart, then finally stopped. Still, no one moved for a while. Akiko was the first one to stand up. Then Janey's mom joined her, and they all stood, brushing the reddish soil from their clothing. Without speaking, they walked down the cane row single file, with Mom carrying Michael.

Janey realized, now that she was not terrified and trying to run, that the cane plants were so big there was just barely enough room between them to walk. The row seemed longer, too, as though they would never emerge into the sunshine.

Finally, Janey could see the end of the row, and she followed her mother out of the field. Behind her, Akiko walked without speaking. There were three other cars parked along the road now, and Janey saw other people were making their way back out of the cane. Below, the smoke rising from the harbor had thickened into a black curtain that hid everything.

Akiko ran forward. Janey watched her turn one way, then the other, her face eager. When her shoulders sank, Janey knew without looking that Akiko's parents hadn't arrived—nor had her uncle and aunt.

"Your parents will come soon, Akiko," Janey called. Akiko met her eyes, but she didn't say anything. Janey glanced at her mother. She was still holding Michael, only with difficulty now. He was squirmy and trying to get down. Janey sidled close and tried to get him to smile at her. When he wouldn't, she reluctantly looked out over the harbor again.

"Where's Pokey?" Michael demanded suddenly.

Janey winced. *Pokey is probably all right,* she told herself, trying to believe it.

CHAPTER SIX

Janey sat on the sun-warmed hood of the Buick, her feet dangling down over the slats of the silvery chrome grill. Her father would want to wash the car once they were all home and together, she was sure. There were red Christmas berries caught in the grill's slots, she noticed, and she bent to pull the twigs out.

Akiko had settled on the running board. Her knees were up beneath her chin, and she sat still without speaking for so long that Janey began to think she had fallen asleep. But then, she opened her eyes and looked down at the harbor with such sadness in her eyes that Janey wanted to tell her that her parents were all right—that everything would work out, some-how. But how could she say that? How could anyone say it?

"But my daddy *is* all right," she whispered to her-self, over and over when her mother wasn't close enough to hear her. "He has to be all right."

Cars kept coming up the dirt road, raising a thin

spatter of red dirt from their rear tires. Some of the people's faces were slightly familiar to Janey—but most were complete strangers. Her mother said hello to two or three people, but Janey could tell Mom felt as alone as she did. Her card-playing friends all lived in Honolulu, the wives of the men her father worked with. And they were casual friends, not close ones. Janey sighed. They just hadn't lived here long enough to have real friends. She felt a long, aching wrench of homesickness. If this had happened in Kansas, they would have been surrounded by people who knew her father, who were as worried as she and her mother were. Tilly would have held her hand without anyone having to ask.

A car pulled up in front of them, and the man driving it parked at a careless angle, then got out. His wife climbed out of the passenger side, and they went together to stand and look down at the harbor. Janey could hear the woman crying and the low murmur of the man's voice as he tried to comfort her.

People everywhere were talking. A group of Japanese people stood off to one side, speaking very quietly. Their sideward glances let Janey know they were worried about people being angry at them for the attack—just the way Miss Watanabe had seemed at the concert.

Janey glanced at Akiko. She was standing close to the car, her eyes down. Janey said her name, but she didn't look up. After a second, Akiko got back into the car and closed the door. Janey saw her mother glance at Akiko, then meet Janey's eyes for an instant. Tilting her head, Mom gestured for Janey to follow her.

Janey walked with her mother across the road and approached a crowd of people surrounding a gray Ford. A man stood next to the car, a map spread out on the hood. "You can see where the airfields are," he was saying. "If you have relatives near any of them, you can give up on getting in touch, even once you get back home. They are asking civilians to stay off the phones. Military use only."

"They told us all to get out," a woman off to the side said loudly enough that Janey turned to look at her. She had curl rags tied into her hair and she was wearing a bathrobe.

"First Governor Poindexter was on the radio declaring a state of emergency and martial law," the man with the map was saying. "Then the military police drove through our neighborhood with loudspeakers and—"

"They banged on our door," a woman interrupted. "Just about broke it in. Said they were clearing the whole peninsula."

Janey's mother stepped closer, and Janey followed, trying to hear everything that was being said. One woman said that the *Arizona,* one of the biggest battleships, had been sunk, with most of the sailors trapped aboard. "They are still picking people out of the water all over the harbor," she added. "Alive and dead and all covered with oil. Some have terrible burns, I imagine."

Janey felt a wave of nausea go through her body. Swimming in the oil-layered water amid the flames would be terrifying. She stood very still, imagining what it would be like to be trapped on a sinking battleship, the water coursing down the narrow passageways. She turned to look back at the Buick. Akiko had gotten out and was sitting on the running board again.

"Akiko!" Janey gestured at her to come.

Akiko stood up and crossed the road, keeping her head down and her eyes on the ground. "Yes, Janey?" Akiko asked politely.

Janey leaned close. "Don't you want to hear what's going on?"

Akiko shook her head, her eyes still down. Then she lifted her gaze and nodded. "But my mother said"—she breathed—"that I had to be very careful or they might . . ." She looked around.

For the second time, Janey noticed that the Japanese families were standing farther up the road. Janey thought about the military officer who had seen Akiko in the backseat, and she wondered if Akiko would feel better if she went to stand with the Japanese families. But she obviously didn't know any of them.

Another car pulled up, and a man and two children got out. Everyone rushed toward them, asking for news. The man held his hands out, palms up, and raised his voice for all to hear. "All I know is that my wife is still on base somewhere at Hickam Field and I can't get in there to see if she's all right. The roads are all blocked off by soldiers now. Amy is a cook there. They were serving breakfast when the attack came," he added in a lower voice, and his eyes filled with tears that he brushed away angrily.

"Who did you talk to?" Janey's mother called out.

The man looked at her. "A sailor on his way in to Honolulu with a load of medical supplies."

Everyone nodded. That seemed like a reliable enough source.

"Was Honolulu hit, too?" a woman near Janey asked. Her voice was tight with worry. "Are they . . . invading us?"

Janey felt like someone had hit her in the stomach. The idea of Japanese soldiers coming ashore had never occurred to her. But they might. She had seen newsreels of the war in Europe; the battles were horrible, with men swarming forward, shooting and dying.

"Did anyone say anything about ground troops coming ashore?" a man near the back asked pointedly.

The first man shrugged. "No one seemed to know anything about what was going on in Honolulu or on the windward side of the island. Or anything else, really. No one knows what to think."

People began to talk again, their voices angry, frightened, their faces tight and uneasy. Janey glanced at Akiko. "Your aunt and uncle live in Honolulu?" Janey asked.

Akiko nodded, but didn't speak. After a few seconds, she turned away and stared down at the smoke rising from Pearl Harbor. Then she cleared her throat. "All my cousins, all my friends live in Honolulu. I go to school there."

Janey blinked back sudden tears. How could this have happened? How could there ever be war anywhere? It was just too awful to not know if her father was all right, to have to worry and wait like this. Janey glanced at her mother, who was still standing with Michael in her arms, her head tilted as she listened to the people around her talking about what had happened and what they should do next. Janey felt her eyes stinging, and she touched her mother's sleeve. "I'm going back to the car," she managed to say in an even voice.

"All right," her mother said, then looked past her. "Akiko? Will you two stay together, please? I just want to see if anyone knows anything more about Hickam Field."

Akiko looked startled, but she nodded, and Janey walked back across the road, Akiko following her a few steps back.

"I wanted to get away from everyone," Janey said when they got to the car.

"I also prefer to cry by myself," Akiko said. She gestured to the running board, and Janey sat down heavily, expecting Akiko to sit beside her. But she didn't. Instead, she walked away a few steps, then stood with her back to Janey, blocking the view of anyone who might glance across the road.

At first, Janey just sat still, but the tears for her father welled up in her eyes again. She told herself it was silly to cry when she didn't even know if he was hurt. She tried biting her lip. She swallowed hard ten or twelve times, but nothing helped. She started crying, anyway.

She tried to be quiet. No one on this hillside was without worry and fear; why should they have to listen to her crying? But after a minute or two the tears took over and she cried hard, her shoulders shaking. Akiko did not turn around, not even to glance at her. After what felt like an hour, the tears slowed and Janey sniffled, wiping at her eyes and dabbing the tears from her cheeks with her sweater sleeve.

"I think your mother is coming back this way," Akiko said over her shoulder.

"Thanks," Janey said, sniffling. She did not want to upset her mother, or Michael. Especially Michael. He understood all this even less than she did, and he was scared enough without seeing that she was sobbing.

Janey stood up and rubbed her eyes one last time, stepping to the side so that she could see past Akiko's back and across the road. Her mother was heading toward the car, but slowly. She stood in one group of people, then walked to join another a little closer to the car. She looked up once and waved, but was far enough away that Janey was sure she couldn't see her flushed face or the wet streaks down her cheeks.

Akiko kept her back turned until Janey said her name. "Thanks, Akiko," she said, and was surprised that her voice sounded almost normal.

Akiko turned to face her. "You are most welcome, Janey." She didn't exactly smile, but she looked less guarded.

"Your turn?" Janey joked.

Akiko shook her head. "I already cried—sitting in the car before you motioned me over there. Janey, I am truly scared." The last sentence seemed to push its way past Akiko's lips, as though she hadn't meant to say it at all.

"Me too," Janey said.

"Where do you go to school?" Akiko asked.

"Sacred Heart," Janey told her. "My mother is Catholic, even though we almost never go to church."

Akiko looked at her, still without really smiling. "I go to a Japanese school. My parents want me to speak our language well and marry an educated man."

Janey nodded. "My mother says it's good for girls

to go to college—that's the best place to meet men with good futures."

"Did your mother go to college?" Akiko asked, her eyes intent.

Janey shook her head. "No. But she wants me to."

"You should go," Akiko said, and there was no mistaking the intensity in her voice.

"You want to, don't you?" Jane said.

Akiko nodded, a tiny movement. "Yes."

"I guess I do, too. My grades are good enough when I study hard. Will your parents let you?"

"I don't think so," Akiko replied. "My uncle is trying to convince them. He is more modern than my father."

"My grandpa says college money is wasted on a girl. He says my folks should save up to put Michael through some east coast college. He says I should just look for a man who is like my father, patient and kind and funny."

"My father is like that, too. He is most generous with my mother and always patient with his children. He is just not very . . . modern," Akiko finished, her voice low. Then she sighed. "He is old-fashioned with my brothers, too. It is not just with me."

Janey tipped her head, surprised. "I've never seen your brothers."

"I am the youngest by twelve years. My four brothers are all grown."

Janey risked a smile. "My best friend, Tilly, is the youngest of eleven kids."

Akiko's eyes widened. "Eleven?"

Janey nodded. "Her oldest sister is twenty-two years older than she is."

Akiko looked properly amazed. "Tilly lives in Pearl City?"

Janey felt her smile fade. "No. I wish she did."

Akiko looked sympathetic. "Honolulu, then? Will your mother let you take the train to visit? My old-fashioned father will not let me go alone."

"I don't think my mother would let me, either," Janey told her. "But Tilly lives in Kansas, not Honolulu."

Akiko's eyes widened again. "Kansas? That is on the great American Plains."

"It's hot in the summer and cold in the winter, and the land is as flat as"—Janey hesitated, searching for something that was flat enough to describe how flat Kansas really was—"as flat as a taro field," she said finally. "But it stretches as far as you can see in every direction."

Akiko drew in a little breath. "And snow?"

"Just about deep enough to bury the house some winters."

Akiko exhaled, and Janey could see her trying to imagine it. "Snow sounds very beautiful," Akiko said politely.

Janey smiled. "It is, unless you have to shovel it."

Janey G. Blue   69

"Shovel it?" Akiko said. She opened the rear door of the Buick and got out her cloth bag, then faced Janey, holding it. "Why would you shovel snow?"

Janey explained as Akiko listened carefully. "But you have no ocean?" she asked, when Janey was finished.

"No ocean," Janey affirmed.

"I cannot imagine no ending to the land, no sea," Akiko said quietly.

Janey turned to stare out at the smoky haze that hid the harbor and Hickam Field and most of Pearl City now. "It's hard for me to get used to the idea that all that water is out there."

"Listen!" a man shouted over the murmur of other voices.

Janey flinched, and Akiko whirled around. The adults fell completely silent. There, in the distance, was the sound of a plane engine droning. Janey tried to spot it but couldn't. Across the road, Janey's mom ran awkwardly toward them, carrying Michael in a bear hug. "Get back into the cane!"

Akiko turned, and this time she led the way into the rows of cane. Janey followed close behind her, glancing back to make sure her mother was managing Michael's weight without stumbling as they ran. The sound of the plane increased until Janey knew it was straight overhead and flying low.

CHAPTER SEVEN

Sitting beside her breathless mother, with Michael crying quietly, Janey listened carefully. It was a single plane, not a wave of bombers. "Only one," she said aloud. "This time it's just one plane."

"I think so," her mother answered.

Akiko nodded.

They all continued to listen, and even Michael quieted so they could hear better. "Is it circling?" Janey asked as the sound of the engine got louder again. "Is it looking for us?"

Janey's mother made a small sound, and Janey realized that Michael was staring at her, his eyes wide and his mouth open. "Mommy said he was just going past."

Janey took his hands. "She's right. I just asked because I'm scared."

"Me, too," Michael said, nodding slowly, staring into her eyes. Janey felt awful. Her little brother had spent the last few hours silent and terrified, and now she had made it even worse.

"Japanese soldiers would not look for women and children to harm," Akiko said firmly and quietly.

"Are you Japanese?" Michael asked.

Akiko nodded, then shook her head. "I'm American, but my family is from Japan. Japanese are honorable people."

"Okay," Michael said softly, and some of the terror went out of his eyes. Janey saw her mother blow Akiko a silent kiss over the top of Michael's head.

"It's coming back!"

The shout came from somewhere off to their right. There were people hidden all through the cane now, all over the mountainside. Janey felt her heart speed up again. The droning sound of the plane engine was coming closer again. If it wasn't a bomber, what was it doing? Maybe it wasn't a Japanese airplane. "Could it be an American plane?" she asked out loud.

"Maybe," Mom answered. "If they didn't all get destroyed on the ground in that first wave of the attack." Janey heard the unsteadiness in her mother's voice and knew she was remembering the rows and rows of planes at Hickam Field. There were three or four other airfields, she was sure, even though she couldn't remember all of the names. Ewa Field was on the side of Pearl Harbor opposite Hickam. The others were on the other side of the island.

"What was the name of the other place Daddy

worked?" she asked her mother, trying to keep her mind off the increasingly loud drone of the airplane overhead. "The one when we first came."

"Bellows?" Mom said. "Bellows Field?"

"Weren't there lots of planes there?"

Mom nodded. "This one could be American, Janey. But we're going to stay hidden until it's gone."

Janey let out a long breath. She could feel her own pulse at the base of her jaw. "I just wanted to know if we had to be scared or not." Her mother didn't answer, and they all listened to the sound of the throbbing engine overhead. Was it circling? It had to be. Otherwise it'd be gone by now.

"I'm hungry," Michael said.

Akiko picked up her cloth bag. "I have tangerines and poi."

Janey started to make a face at the mention of poi, then realized how rude that might seem, so she pretended to yawn instead. A second later, as Akiko opened the bag and took out perfect, deep orange tangerines, Janey's stomach clenched and she realized how hungry she was.

"Thank you very much," Mom said gratefully. "I'm hungry and thirsty, both."

"Me too!" Michael said as he took his tangerine and began to peel away the loose, stringy skin. Janey's mouth flooded with saliva at the scent of the fruit. Akiko handed her one.

The sound of the plane was diminishing but, as they ate, it began to get louder again. "It *is* circling," Mom said, using her hankie as a napkin for herself and Michael.

Her hand was shaking, Janey noticed. Pulling in a deep breath, Janey tried to calm herself. Whatever it was doing, this plane wasn't dropping bombs or strafing the ground with bullets—not yet, anyway. She felt her stomach tighten at the involuntary thought.

Akiko pulled a jar of poi out of her bag. It was a light purplish color, and Janey felt her stomach tighten another notch. "No thank you," she said politely.

"Janey hates poi," Michael said.

Akiko nodded solemnly, but Janey saw her press her lips together as though she was offended. "I'm sorry," Janey said quickly. "It's just that I'm not used to it and I—"

"Don't apologize," Akiko said quickly. "I hate it too. My mother is the one who likes Hawaiian food." She extended the jar to Janey's mother.

"Perhaps later," Mom said. She didn't like poi much, either, Janey knew, in part because everyone dipped fingers into the poi bowl. Mom was prissy about that kind of thing.

"It's going away," Michael said. "The plane is going away."

Janey glanced upward even though there was nothing to see except the grassy cane leaves overhead.

He was right: The engine sound was dimming into nothingness this time. There was a moment of complete silence, then someone behind them started to cheer. It spread through the cane, a hundred or more voices joining in a cry of relief and happiness. Janey heard rustling all around them as people got up and made their way back into the open.

The harbor was still aflame, but the breeze had blown back the smoke a little and the destruction was visible for the first time. The massive warships had been beaten and battered. Several of them lay cock-eyed in the water now, slanting heavily to one side. Janey could see men crawling over them like ants. *How many people have been killed?* she wondered, then pushed the thought as far away as she could. Her father had not been on one of the ships. Maybe most of the bombs had been dropped on the warships.

Most the ships were on fire; it looked as though even the harbor itself was burning. "How can the water be burning?" Michael whispered.

Janey's mother pointed. "See how black it looks? It's a layer of oil floating on the surface—from the ships' fuel tanks."

The smoke was thinning everywhere. For the first time, Janey could catch clear glimpses of Hickam Field. What she could see scared her. There were hulks of planes lying in shattered rows. They were too far away to make out what the people were doing, but

Janey saw men milling around by the hundreds. The buildings around the airfield were on fire too. "It's awful," Janey breathed.

Her mother put her hand on her shoulder and sighed. "It is. And I don't know how to tell when it's safe to go back down."

Janey looked at the scattered crowds of people reforming along the road, all of them looking down toward the harbor again. She heard a car engine start. The driver eased it out of the uneven line of parked cars, then started down the road, back toward Pearl City.

"Watch Michael for a few minutes, Janey, please," Mom said. "I want to go hear what other people think about this." She bent to look into Michael's face. "Be good. I'll be right back."

Michael nodded solemnly. "I will."

Janey gestured back at the Buick. "Want to go sit down again?"

"All right. We can see better from over there," Akiko answered, starting back across the road. Janey took her brother's hand and led him along. He was tired, she could tell. He was taking tiny steps and rubbing his eyes with his free hand.

"Want to take a nap in the backseat?" Janey asked him.

Michael shook his head. "No. I'm not sleepy."

"Okay," Janey answered him. "Then sit up here

with me." She lifted him up onto the fender. He flailed his arms and shook his head. "I want to stay down."

Janey sighed. "Fine. I'll open the back door and you can crawl in and take a nap if you want to." She slid down and opened the car door, then watched until Michael settled himself on the running board and began drawing in the red dirt with a stick he'd found. Only then did she crawl back up on the hood. Akiko joined her, sitting on the other side. The metal was almost too hot from the afternoon sun, but it felt good in a way, too, comforting, like a hearth fire.

"How long before we can go back, do you think?" Akiko asked.

Janey shrugged, then smiled. "You aren't that shy, are you? You just pretended to be." Akiko ducked her head, and Janey was instantly sorry she had teased her. "I just meant you're getting more friendly," she said quickly. "My friend Tilly almost never relaxes around anyone except her own family or me."

Akiko didn't answer, but Janey could see her cheeks flushing. "I meant it as a compliment, Akiko," Janey said.

Akiko looked up. "My grandmother says I am much too modern, too forward."

Janey wasn't sure what to say. "My grandparents back in Kansas are old-fashioned, too." She paused. "I miss them a lot."

"I love my grandmother," Akiko said, and she met

Janey's eyes. "I am not shy. I am afraid. Afraid these people will decide all Japanese are their enemies. All the Japanese here are afraid of this."

Janey wasn't sure what to say. Akiko had started to say something like this before, but now she was saying it very clearly, and her direct gaze was almost a challenge.

"I know you aren't my enemy," Janey told her. "But that soldier . . ." Janey trailed off, unable to say what she meant.

"Yes," Akiko said. "He called me a 'little Jap girl.' A lot of people are going to think as he does."

Janey leaned to check on Michael. She caught a glimpse of his trouser leg disappearing as he climbed into the backseat. She sighed, glad he wasn't going to get crabby and fussy. She held a finger to her lips and then whispered, "I think Michael will nap if we're quiet." Akiko nodded to show she had heard. Then she climbed up onto the hood and rested her back against the windshield. Janey hesitated, then climbed up beside her. They sat looking at the devastation in the harbor. "I don't think any of the taro fields are on fire," Janey whispered. "I mean, there's no smoke coming from that side of the peninsula."

Akiko narrowed her eyes, staring at the areas that showed through the drifting smoke. "I just can't understand why my parents weren't there. I can see our houses."

Janey sat up straight. "Can you see your parents outside? I can't make out anything."

Akiko squinted. "No. It's just too far."

Janey waited as a dense trail of smoke drifted across the land, then leaned forward again. "I can see a car in front of your house. It's parked crooked. . . ."

Akiko stood up and shaded her eyes. "I see it. It's probably someone at your house. Your father?"

"Only if he borrowed someone's car—the lieutenant's jeep came for him this morning. Or maybe it's Mr. Wilkins," Janey said, suddenly remembering. "He was going to come pick Dad up at eight to go fishing."

Akiko didn't answer, but she leaned forward, squinting again.

Janey stared, blinking when the smoke shifted and blurred the view again. The harbor was full of smaller boats, surrounded by a tangle of people, trucks, and cars, but the streets in Pearl City were empty. She watched for a long time, then squeezed her eyes shut. Maybe Mr. Wilkins had just left his car and gotten a ride with someone else. Or maybe it was someone else's car and . . .

A sudden explosion from the harbor stopped Janey mid-thought. She realized she had jumped off the car hood and was standing tensely, ready to run. "Is there a plane?" she whispered.

Akiko was on the ground too, looking over the arch of the long hood at her. "I don't see one."

"Ammunition," a man called out, and the murmuring quieted as people hushed to listen to him. "It's ammunition from one of the boats. The shells are exploding in the fires."

The murmuring rose again, and Janey saw her mother glance over at her, then turn her attention back to the woman she was talking to. A car rolled up, the driver slowing to a crawl as he wove his way forward through the parked cars. When he stopped, he got out and raised both hands into the air.

"I've got a shortwave radio!" he announced. Instantly, every person in the crowd turned to face him, silent and waiting.

"They're saying the attack was probably the first wave of an invasion force," the man went on. "They said we can expect a landing soon. The military is preparing now."

"Is that much certain?" a man called out, and Janey waited for the answer, holding her breath.

"Nothing is certain," the man admitted. "But it looks like an invasion, and—"

"Why would the Japs invade us?" a woman's voice interrupted him. "Look at how many Japanese we have living here." A rising tide of murmurs kept Janey from being able make sense out of anything else that was said.

"Maybe some of our Japanese are spying. Maybe that's how the bombers knew where the airfields were, where they should attack," one man said loudly.

No one spoke, but Janey saw people staring at the group of Japanese families down the road. The crowd looked troubled, not angry, as though the man had said something that hadn't occurred to them before, that had raised a question for which they had no answer. People shifted from one foot to the other, and for a long moment no one spoke. Then a woman raised her voice. "I have Japanese neighbors. There are no finer people—they have been my friends for years."

A murmur swelled in the crowd. Most of the voices Janey could hear were thoughtful, agreeing with what the woman had said. But people continued to glance down the road. Janey held her breath, feeling a tension in the air that scared her almost as much as the bombs had. She glanced at Akiko. Her face was pale, her eyes wide.

CHAPTER EIGHT

Without saying a word, people in the crowd began to drift away, turning their backs on the man who had made the announcement. Akiko looked stunned. She crawled into the backseat, turning to slide past Michael. He was asleep, sprawled on the wide seat. She sat against the far door and slumped down.

Janey got in the front, leaving the door ajar so that the clunking of the catch wouldn't wake her brother. She got up on her knees to look over the seat at Akiko's bowed head. "They're just scared, talking like that," she said.

After a moment's silence, Akiko nodded without speaking.

"I mean, they *were* Japanese planes and soldiers and . . ." Janey trailed off, then took a long breath. "People are just scared and they—"

"My mother said terrible things might happen," Akiko interrupted, raising her chin. "She told me to keep quiet—to be invisible until she and my father came."

"People will understand that you're American," Janey said, trying to believe it. "Half the people on Oahu are from somewhere else. And the Hawaiians put up with all of us coming to their islands."

Akiko nodded somberly. "But the Portuguese or the Filipinos or the Chinese have not crossed an ocean to drop bombs on us, have they? Only the Japanese." Akiko said nothing more for a long moment. Then she looked out the window. "I wish my parents would come."

Janey leaned forward. "I am so scared my father is hurt," she said around a jagged lump that had suddenly filled her throat.

Akiko reached forward, and they clasped hands. "My mother and father should have been there, in the taro. What could have happened?" Akiko covered her mouth with one hand, then took a long, uneven breath. "What will happen if the Japanese soldiers invade? People will shoot at anyone who looks Japanese. My father and brothers—"

"Maybe they won't invade," Janey said quickly. The idea of an invasion was more than she could stand. She sobbed, a low sound of fear escaping from her lips before she could stop it.

Michael's eyes fluttered open. He pedaled his feet until he found a way to scoot himself around, then wriggled upright. His eyes were wide, and he stood up and leaned forward to hug Janey. Then he saw the people gathered across the road. "Where's Mom?" he asked. Janey tried to wipe away her tears, but he had leaned back to study her face. "What's wrong, Janey?"

"Nothing," Janey told him, glancing at Akiko. "I just got upset. I . . ." She stopped herself from saying that she was worried about the war, worried about Dad, scared of another attack, an invasion. . . .

"Did you notice the car?" Mom asked, startling Janey as she opened the driver's door. "It's more or less in front of our house."

Janey nodded. "Is it Mr. Wilkins's?"

Her mother shrugged. "I don't know. Or maybe your father borrowed a car to come home." She straightened her skirt, then looked at Janey. "We all need to stay as calm as we can," she said gently. "Michael?" She turned and aimed her voice over the seat. "Do you want to ride up here?"

Michael launched himself at the back of the seat, climbing like a monkey, clunking Janey in the head with his shoe as he flopped into his usual position between them. On any other day, Janey would have yelped so that Mom would tell Michael to be more careful. Today, she just reached up to make sure he didn't tumble onto the floor as he slid down.

"I think we should go home and see if we can find your dad and Akiko's parents. What do you think?"

"Yes!" Janey said.

"Yes," Akiko said more quietly.

"I want Daddy," Michael said, jumping up again.

"Akiko?" Janey's mother said as she coaxed Michael into sitting down. "Make sure both those doors are closed tight, will you? And Janey, close yours, please."

Janey leaned outward to grab the chrome handle and dragged the heavy door toward her. It closed solidly. One back door slammed shut, then the other.

"Ready?" Janey's mother asked.

"Ready!" Michael answered her.

"Yes, ma'am," Akiko said from the backseat.

Janey watched her mother turn the key, then put the car in gear. They slid forward smoothly, gracefully clearing the cars on both sides.

"All right," Mom said as they drove slowly past the groups of people and parked cars. "We'll just go home long enough to find our families, then we'll all come back up here." Janey noticed that her voice was shaking.

"Most of the people are staying," Janey said, her voice coming up at the end as though it were a question.

Mom cleared her throat. "I know. But some of them thought that if there was going to be an invasion, it would come tonight. And I want to be"—she paused and pulled in a careful breath—"I want us all to be with our families by then." She half turned. "Akiko, if we can't find your parents, if we miss them somehow, you will stay with us until we do. Is that all right?"

Akiko leaned forward, and Janey stretched up to see her pretty face. "Yes, ma'am," she answered.

"I do have a favor to ask," Mom added.

"Yes, ma'am?" Akiko answered, and her voice was tentative.

"Teach my daughter some manners, will you?"

Akiko smiled a little.

"I'm so glad I left your father that note," Mom told Janey as she made the first turn downhill and speeded up a little. "I told him we'd be back as soon as we could. Maybe he's just been waiting for us."

Janey looked out the window. This road had far fewer people on it. "Akiko wrote one, too," she told her mother.

"Good." Mom turned to look at a group of farmers standing beside their truck, looking down at the harbor. The back of the truck was open, and Janey saw piles of green stalks with strangely swollen roots.

"Fresh taro," Akiko said from the backseat. "They must have a field and sell it like my parents do."

Janey turned around in the seat to see. "Taro? To make poi?"

Akiko smiled and nodded. "Though why anyone wants to make it is a mystery."

Janey twisted back around. She longed for this to be a normal day, a day when she could ask Akiko how poi was made. On normal days, she was curious about everything. But today, nothing mattered except getting home and finding her father there, safe and well.

Mom wheeled the Buick around one sharp turn, then another. The lower they got, the fewer people they saw. Mom pressed the gas pedal a little harder, speeding up again. Every few seconds, Janey noticed, her mother was ducking forward, trying to see the sky out the windshield.

"I'll keep watch, Mom," Janey said quietly.

Her mother looked startled, then she nodded. "Good. Watch all four directions, not just the one they came from this morning. Some of the people thought they would fly in another way to surprise us next time."

"I'll watch from back here." Akiko said it very quietly, as though she wasn't sure she should speak up at all.

"Thanks," Janey said.

"Terrific," her mother added.

Janey sat up straight enough to see that Akiko was riding backward, up on her knees, to get a good view out the rear window.

"Brave girls," Janey's mother said, and speeded up a little more. "You are both brave girls."

"I'll watch, too," Michael said, and Janey reached to touch his cheek. He hadn't cried even as much as she and Akiko had.

The fields slid past, and they turned onto the government road toward Pearl City. The smoke drifted across the landscape, and it was bitter-smelling, stinging Janey's nose and eyes. Michael coughed every few seconds, but he didn't complain.

"Oh, no," Mom said suddenly.

Janey turned to look forward. There were two military jeeps parked in the road, sideways. Mom braked, slowing to a smooth stop. "I am going back to find my husband," Mom shouted out the window.

A soldier shook his head and got out of the jeep. "I can't let anyone back in this area, ma'am."

Janey saw her mother's hands begin to tremble on the wheel.

"You don't understand. We will only be in the area long enough to find my husband and Akiko's parents and—"

The soldier snapped into a straighter posture and he bent to look in at the backseat. When he straightened up again, his face was set, expressionless. "Ma'am, I can't make any exceptions. I have orders."

"But what harm can there be in us going back to our own house for five minutes and—"

"Ma'am," the soldier interrupted again. "I can't let you pass."

"My husband is probably waiting for us!" Mom exploded. "We could see a car from the mountain slopes. We were up in the cane fields and—"

"I can't do it, ma'am," the soldier repeated.

"We have a neighbor's girl with us," Mom went

on, ignoring the man's stony stare. "Her parents are probably frantic to find her."

The soldier shook his head. "No exceptions, ma'am," he repeated.

Michael whimpered and looked like he was about to cry. Janey reached out to put her arm around his shoulders. "Don't cry," she whispered. "It's all right." But she knew it wasn't. This soldier was not going to let them pass. He didn't care how desperate they were, and he didn't care about her father or Akiko's parents.

"You'll have to turn the car around here," the soldier said firmly.

"I can't," Janey heard her mother say.

"I can back it around for you if you like, ma'am," the soldier said quietly. His lips were pressed into a tight line.

"Where do you recommend I take these children?" Mom demanded suddenly, her voice shaking.

"Ma'am, that's up to you. But I can't let you back in here yet. Maybe tomorrow," he added, but he sounded so uncertain that Janey saw her mother's knuckles go white on the steering wheel.

"Do you know where they took wounded men from Hickam Field?" she asked in a low voice.

Janey felt her heartbeat slow down, then speed up.

The soldier shook his head again. "Some infirmaries have been set up on Ford Island and elsewhere.

Some wounded were taken into Honolulu."

Janey's mother let out a long breath. "Is there any chance of me being able to drive onto the airfield to see if my husband . . ."

She trailed off because the soldier was already shaking his head. "No. I'm sorry."

"Can I still get into Honolulu?" Mom asked. All the anger was gone from her voice now. She was nearly whispering.

This time, the soldier frowned. "Honolulu has been bombed, ma'am—that's what the radio said, anyway. Now, if you need help turning that car around—"

"Janey, hang on tight," Mom said clearly, interrupting the soldier. "Akiko—you too, please." Janey put one arm around Michael and pushed herself upward to glance into the backseat. Akiko was still facing backward, but she had braced her feet against the back of the front seat and was hanging on to the edge of the window well with both hands.

"Ready," Janey said to her mother, and the tires squealed as the car shot backward. Janey saw the soldier's look of astonishment and she almost smiled as her mother skidded the car around in a perfectly controlled slow-slide half turn, then stopped. Then Mom took a deep breath and shifted it into first gear, gently touched the gas pedal, and started out slowly.

"How dare he tell me I can't go to my own home!" Mom fumed as she drove. Then her voice softened. "I know they have orders. I'm just worried about your dad." Janey nodded, and they exchanged a glance over Michael's head. "But it's just worry," Mom said a little louder. "I'm sure he's fine."

"Where are we going to go?" Michael asked.

Janey glanced up at her mother. Neither of them spoke.

CHAPTER NINE

For a long time, Janey's mother just drove, slowly, without speaking. Janey watched the sky, shifting her eyes from one horizon to the other, then back. She glanced at Akiko, who still rode backward, staring out the rear window.

As they came to the edge of Pearl City's business district, Janey heard her mother sigh. "I don't have a lot of gas left," she said aloud. "And I imagine it's pretty hard to buy gas right now. Probably impossible."

Janey turned. "Are we going to go to Honolulu? He said it had been bombed."

Her mother nodded. "But he didn't sound all that sure. I just wanted to check the hospitals, whatever they have set up to help people find each other. And . . ." Her voice failed, and Janey glanced at her brother. He was fiddling with the buttons on his shirt, and if he had heard Mom sounding as if she was about to cry, he acted as if he hadn't.

"I have relatives in Honolulu," Akiko said from

the backseat. She sounded happy and excited. "We could go to any of their houses."

Mom shook her head. "Thank you, Akiko, but no. Not tonight, anyway. Everyone up in the cane fields seemed to think that an invasion would start there, near Honolulu. So even if your relatives wouldn't mind us staying until we could go home, even if my husband is there, I can't take you three straight into danger without enough gas in the car to make it back to the mountains if we ran into trouble."

Janey ducked to look out the window, scanning the sky for planes. "What if there wasn't an attack, Mom?"

Mom shrugged. "Then there wasn't. But I can't take the chance." She sighed. "I guess we go back to the cane fields. I can't think of anywhere safer. I just thought . . ." She trailed off. "Well, I just thought we could get back to our houses, that's all. And when I saw that car, I thought . . ." She trailed off again and pounded the steering wheel with her right hand.

Akiko was silent, her face blank and her mouth set in a straight line as she stared out one side window, then the other, then through the back window again.

Reminded that she was supposed to be looking, too, Janey squinted to sharpen her vision against the low afternoon sun. Then she blinked and swallowed hard. There was a speck on the horizon. She held her breath, watching. It was getting closer. "I see a plane," she said quietly.

Her mother speeded up. "How far away?"

"Pretty far," Janey said. "It still just looks like a bird or something. But it's coming more or less this way."

"Only one?"

Janey squinted. "I think so."

"Yes, only one," Akiko said from the backseat. She was on Janey's side now, bent over low to see more sky out the side window.

Janey bit at her lip. "I still only see one."

"Is it much closer?"

Janey shook her head. "Not much. It's way off."

"Then I think we'll be up in the hills before it gets too close," Mom said.

Janey nodded, hoping it was true. "It's not dropping bombs yet or shooting," she added.

Michael was sitting close to her, peering out the window. "I see the plane!" he said.

"Help your sister keep an eye on it," Mom said.

Janey glanced at her. Her hands were still shaky on the wheel, but even so she was driving better than most people ever would, smooth and fast, taking the turns perfectly.

For a long time, Mom was silent and Janey concentrated on the plane. It wasn't coming straight at them, she realized. And as it got closer, angling off toward Pearl City, she noticed it didn't have a rising sun painted on the side. "I think it's an American plane," Janey said as they rounded the last turn and her mother slowed to pass the parked cars and crowds of people again.

"Jeeps," Akiko said.

"Where?" Janey turned to look at her. Akiko pointed, and Janey followed the gesture.

The jeeps were parked in the cane fields. They had been driven in at an angle, breaking off some of the tall stalks beneath their wheels.

Janey felt her mother hesitate, then brake, parking opposite the jeeps. "Can you see the soldiers?"

Janey shook her head, but Akiko spoke up again. "There!"

Janey and her mother turned around to look through the back window. Michael struggled to his feet to lean on the seat back. "I see them," he said quietly.

Janey's mother opened her door. "Wait here. If you get out, stay right beside the car."

For a moment, they all sat still, watching her walk away. Then Janey opened her door and slid to the ground. Akiko did the same. "Do you want to get out, Michael?" Janey asked her brother. He shook his head. "Are you sleepy?"

He shook his head, then nodded. "I'm hungry, too."

Janey sighed as she watched her brother lie down across the front seat. She closed the door gently, glad he was going to sleep again. She was tired and hot and hungry, and she felt like she was about to cry again.

"Please get into your vehicles!"

Janey started at the sudden shout.

"Get into you cars and prepare to follow the lead jeep!" the soldier shouted. "Get into your vehicles now!"

Janey blinked. What was going on now? If her mother had known about this, they might not have come back.

"Where are we going?" a man shouted, but the soldier either didn't hear or pretended not to. He turned without so much as glancing at the people again, and got into one of the jeeps. Starting the engine, he pulled back onto the road and drove forward past the cane fields.

"Into your vehicles!" came another shout, this one a growling bass voice. "Please, folks, let's just get going here."

Janey saw a tense-faced soldier standing in the middle of the road. He pointed at a Filipino family. "Do you have a vehicle?" He shouted the words slowly and with an exaggerated pronunciation, as if he were talking to small children.

"We walked from our farm," the man replied in perfect English.

"Then get in with someone else, please. We have about five miles to go."

"Where are we going?" the man asked again.

"Sir, this is an evacuation, executed pursuant to orders under military emergency. Now get into your car, or find one to ride in with another family, please."

Janey saw her mother walking back toward them.

As she passed the Filipino family, she leaned to say something to the man. Janey saw her gesture toward their car, but the man pointed in the opposite direction. Janey's mother nodded and went on. "They are evacuating people," she said.

Janey tilted her head, unsure of what the word meant. "That's what he said." She gestured at the soldier. "But what's *evacuating* mean?"

"They're moving people out of this area," her mother said.

"Why?" Akiko asked. Suddenly, she looked the way she had that morning, remote and angry. "Where are they taking us?"

Janey's mother shook her head. "I'm not sure. No one seemed to know. Somewhere safe for the night, they said."

"Let's go!" the soldier shouted. His face was flushed, and he looked impatient. People slowly started toward their cars, carrying their toddlers and dragging their feet.

"I don't want to go," Akiko said suddenly.

Janey looked at her mother. "I don't, either. Why won't they tell us where they are taking us?"

Janey's mother shook her head. "They're tired and scared, just like the rest of us, I guess. Maybe they have orders not to tell people. I don't know. I think we should go. They know more than the rest of us about where an invasion might come, where we will be safest."

Akiko took a step backward. "I am not going to go with the soldiers," she said.

Janey stared at her, understanding. Akiko's mother had warned her that Japanese people might be treated as enemies, and she was scared. "But they won't let you stay here, will they?" Janey looked at her mother. "Can she stay? Could we all stay here?"

Akiko stepped back once more. "This is my uncle's field. My family will come here when they can." Her voice was quivering, and Janey imagined herself spending a night alone, listening for planes. It would be awful.

Janey's mother stepped forward quickly and put her arm around Akiko's shoulders. "I can't just leave you here. But we'll be among the last to go, all right? If your parents come at the last minute, we'll see them."

Akiko seemed to relax a little, and Janey forced a smile. "It'll be fine," she said aloud. "The soldiers aren't going to do anything to you, and—"

"You cannot promise me that," Akiko interrupted her. "I should have obeyed my mother and stayed at home."

"But what your mother said was silly," Janey burst out, frantic to talk Akiko into going with them.

"Janey!" Mom said. "You're being disrespectful."

Janey looked at Akiko's face and knew instantly that her mother was right. Akiko was offended. "I'm sorry," Janey said quietly.

Akiko nodded, making it into the tiniest motion, then looked away.

"Come on, girls," Janey's mother was saying. "Get in the car and we'll wait for everyone else to get turned around."

Akiko stood still for a second, then slowly walked over to the rear door of the Buick. She put her hand on the handle, but then she hesitated, looking out across the edge of the cane fields. She frowned. "How can the soldiers just drive over the plants like that?"

Janey shrugged. "They're just thinking about other things, I guess. They shouldn't have," she added quickly when she saw the frown deepen on Akiko's face.

"My mother was right," Akiko whispered. "Most of these people are going to think that every Japanese person is their enemy. I see people looking at me."

Janey glanced at her mother, who was sitting in the driver's seat, her feet still sideways, looking out at the flame-spotted harbor. Akiko had made sure she wouldn't be able to hear.

"Well, I don't think so," Janey said in her steadiest voice. "And my mother doesn't."

Akiko looked grim and she shook her head. "All the soldiers look at me like they think I am dangerous."

Janey opened her mouth to argue, but it was impossible. Akiko was scared, so it seemed that way to her. And the first soldier had almost said exactly that. "But you have to come with us and . . ." Janey began, but she never managed to finish her sentence. Akiko suddenly spun and ran across the road, disappearing into the cane.

CHAPTER TEN

For a few seconds, Janey and her mother stood still. Janey stared at the place where Akiko had slipped into the cane field. It was as though the green leaves had swallowed her.

"Catch up with her if you can and try to talk sense into her," Mom said, leaning in to pick up Michael. "Shout when you find her." Janey clambered out of the car, her mother still talking. "I can't just leave her here. I'd be furious if anyone ever did that to you or Michael."

Janey took off running, feeling the prickle of the cane leaves when they brushed her skin. It was harder to avoid the sharp-edged leaves now. The angled, late afternoon sunlight didn't penetrate the leaves overhead the way it had earlier. It was dusky and hard to see, but Janey caught glimpses of Akiko running and tried to keep up. Then, suddenly, her foot caught on something and she fell, hitting the ground so hard that for a second she couldn't get her breath.

Sitting up slowly, Janey peered ahead, but Akiko was out of sight now. Janey tried to see where the cane leaves were still swaying from where Akiko had brushed them, but it just wasn't light enough anymore.

"Akiko?" she called out softly, hoping for an answer, but there wasn't one.

Brushing off her skirt, Janey stood still, wondering what she should do next. Not far off to her right, she heard a rustling in the cane. Smiling, hoping that Akiko had calmed down and was on her way back, Janey started toward the sound, wincing when she put her weight on her right ankle. She had twisted it, she realized, but she kept going, frantic to find Akiko and get back to her mother.

It was hard to find gaps in the row of cane that were big enough for her to slip through, but Janey kept going, stopping now and then to listen for the rustling again and to adjust her direction. "Akiko?" she called out softly as she got closer. "Akiko, can you hear me?"

The rustling stopped abruptly. Janey stilled her breathing. "Akiko?"

There was no answer. The silent seconds ticked past as Janey held her breath, determined to pinpoint the direction when Akiko moved again, even a little. Her ankle was aching, and she ignored the pain to concentrate on listening.

"Janey?" It was her mother's voice, and Janey looked up, not wanting to shout.

"Janey? Are you all right?"

Janey heard a rustle in the cane off to her left. "Akiko?" she whispered. There was no answer.

"Janey?" Mom called again. "Have you found her? Is everything all right?"

Janey bit her lip, starting to get angry. "Akiko? You're scaring my mother," she said in a low voice. "All we're trying to do is help you and keep you safe."

There was a long silence, then, finally, Janey heard a small, frightened voice. "I don't mean to be ungrateful—"

"Akiko!" Janey said sharply. "Where are you?"

The cane rustled, and Janey saw Akiko crawling through the dense leaves. Then she got to her feet.

"Akiko!" Janey burst out, then lowered her voice. "Akiko, you have to come back with me and—"

"I can't, Janey."

Janey stared at her. "You have to. What if they're evacuating people because this is a dangerous place?"

Akiko shook her head. "Why would it be?"

Janey searched for an answer and found she didn't have one. "I don't know. But what if it is?" She took a step toward Akiko and wobbled, setting down her right foot carefully.

"Are you hurt?" Akiko asked.

"I twisted my ankle," Janey told her.

"Oh," Akiko said, reaching out to steady her. "And it's all my fault."

Janey shrugged. It was Akiko's fault in an indirect way, but the last thing Janey wanted to do was make Akiko feel bad. "I could have run slower," she said aloud. "I should have watched where I was going."

Akiko sniffled, and Janey realized that she had been crying again. "We'll find your parents tonight or tomorrow," Janey told her. "I just know it."

Akiko touched Janey's shoulder. "And your father."

"Janey?" Mom shouted. "Janey, answer me!"

"We're fine, Mom!" Janey shouted back, then she looked at Akiko and spoke softly, urgently. "You have to come with us. My mother won't leave you here alone, I know it, and she won't stay because she wants us all to be safe."

"I only wish it was anyone but soldiers leading us," Akiko said, and Janey heard the tenseness coming back into her voice. "They scare me."

"You won't have to talk to them at all. My mother will do it." There was a sudden honking from the road, and Janey heard two men shouting at each other to watch where they were going. The voices softened and fell, and finally apologies were called out, followed by the sound of engines revving.

"Everyone is afraid, Akiko," Janey said. "No one knows what's going on, and no one knows what will happen. But we have to stay together."

"I thought, when I ran, that you would leave me here. I thought your mother would just decide that I was too much trouble."

Janey shook her head. "You don't know my mother. She would never do that to anyone. And she likes you."

"Because she thinks I will teach you to say 'ma'am'?" Akiko said in a serious voice, and it took Janey a long moment to realize that she had made a joke.

"I'm sure that's a big part of it," Janey answered, trying to match Akiko's serious tone.

"If I have to run away again," Akiko said, her voice suddenly fierce, "it will not be because you and your family have not been very good to me. Please remember that."

"Janey?" Mom yelled. "We should get turned around now."

"Coming!" Janey shouted. Then she reached out to take Akiko's hand. "You won't have to run away again. Don't even think about doing that. Now come on, please."

Coming out of the cane, Janey realized how sore her ankle really was. She limped along, and Akiko stayed right beside her, steadying her as they walked. It was almost dark beneath the cane leaves, and as they stepped out into the open again, Janey saw that it was getting dusky.

"Oh, thank heavens," Janey heard her mother say the moment they stepped out of the cane. The sun was sinking, half hidden by the horizon now. There were only eight or ten cars left on the road. The taillights of the ones driving slowly upward into the hills were strung out like a chain of bright beads in the twilight.

"Oh, Akiko," Mom said. "I am so glad to see you." She hugged Akiko with one arm, hoisting Michael higher to keep him from sliding as she bent over.

"I apologize," Akiko said. "I know I have been too much trouble."

"You just scared me a little," Mom said, and Janey felt a surge of pride. So many mothers would have been angry and impatient. Mom was most concerned about Akiko's feelings. Mom hitched Michael higher in her arms. He looked sleepy and was silent.

"Okay, lady!" a male voice shouted from across the road, startling Janey into stepping backward. Her sore ankle made her misstep, and Akiko held her up.

"Are you hurt?" her mother asked.

"She twisted an ankle, and it is my fault," Akiko said unhappily.

"I'm all right, Mom," Janey said quickly. "It's not much of a sprain. I can walk just fine if I limp a little."

"Everyone be careful," Mom said, her voice level and intense. "Just be careful. We need to take care of each other."

"Lady?" the man shouted in a derisive voice from across the road. "Lady, do you suppose you could get in the car and get going with the others now? Do you need help getting it turned around?"

Janey felt her mother stiffen at the insult, but she squared her shoulders and smiled at the soldier. "I think I can manage, sir."

Then she lowered her voice. "I am so tired of men thinking I can't drive decently because I am a woman."

"You drive good," Michael said quietly.

Janey smiled weakly. It was good to hear her mother irritated instead of scared. It was good to hear her brother speak aloud, saying something cute and dear. It made things seem almost normal for a few seconds as they piled into the car.

"Everyone set?" Mom asked, and Janey braced herself, but this time her mother started off slowly, driving so smoothly that the Buick swayed gently like a boat as they made the turn and got headed in the right direction.

"Keep up with the others," the soldier yelled as they passed. Janey's mother nodded politely, then drove on as slowly as she had started. It was only after a few other cars were behind them that she sped up enough to catch up with the line in front of them.

Janey sat quietly in the front seat, watching the lights of the cars in front of them glowing as they snaked in a long line through the cane fields. They made so many turns, it was impossible to tell where they were going, and as the dark of night deepened, the countryside was almost entirely hidden from them. Only the tall cane along the edges of the fields leaped into sight as the headlights flowed across it.

"How much farther?" Michael asked.

Janey's mother reached over and ruffled his hair. "Not much farther at all, I don't think. You can lie down and nap if you want to."

Michael wrinkled his face into a frown. "I'm hungry."

The instant he said it, Janey felt her own stomach cramp. She was hungry. She was incredibly hungry.

The sharp, sweet smell of citrus fruit filled the air a few seconds later. "I still have three tangerines," Akiko said, passing a peeled one to Janey.

"You kids have one each," Janey's mother said. "I'm too busy driving to eat, anyway."

Janey, knowing her mother was just being nice, meant to save some of her tangerine for her, but she crammed the sweet sections of fruit into her mouth so fast, it was gone before she'd realized it.

Michael finished his nearly as fast, then lay down on the seat, curled up between his mother and sister. They drove without talking for a long time. Janey sat still, staring out at the darkness, listening. She couldn't stop listening for plane engines, for men's voices, for gunfire. Finally, ahead of them, the line of cars slowed, then stopped.

"Where are we?" Akiko asked from the backseat. "Can you see anything?"

Janey heard the uneasiness in her voice and wished she knew the answer to her question. But she didn't. "No," she said aloud. "It's too dark."

The night around them seemed oppressive, heavy. Janey stared ahead, then twisted around to look backward. She caught her breath when she saw the glow of distant fires. "Is that the harbor?"

Akiko shifted on the backseat. "I think so. I didn't look back at first and when I did, it looked like that."

"I kept an eye on it," Mom said. "As a way of keeping track of the direction we were headed." She sighed. "That's Pearl Harbor, all right. It'll never be the same, that's for sure."

"Nothing ever will," Janey heard Akiko say.

The line in front of them began to move, and Janey's mother inched the car forward. There was nothing else they could do. They were boxed in by cars on both sides.

"There's something," Janey said, when the headlights of the cars happened to brush across a clay oven built beside a planked-walled building. "Houses, maybe?" she said aloud, but the building looked too big to be a house. Or, if it was that big, it should have been fancier, like the vacation houses outside Pearl City.

"Look at that one," Akiko said quietly.

Janey turned to see another big building flanked by a much smaller one.

"Is that a garage?" Janey wondered aloud. Only rich people had garages—but the building was rough-hewn, like the first one had been. She sat up straight so she could see over the seat. Akiko had pressed herself up against the car door and was staring out the window. They passed one more building, and this time Janey saw a huge chimney set into the wall. Then the darkness closed in again, and there was nothing at all to see except the long, grassy leaves of the sugarcane.

Shouting from ahead of them caught Janey's ear, and she straightened up, blinking. She saw lights shining at them as someone backed his car in a half circle. Then the lights winked out. She rubbed her eyes, staring. People were parking. She could see a few families standing outside their cars. "What is this place?" she murmured.

"I don't know," her mother answered.

"Akiko, have you ever been here?" Janey asked, sitting up straight to look into the backseat.

"No." Akiko shook her head, her eyes wide when headlights swept across their faces. "But I know what it is. It's a sugar plantation. Those houses are for the workers. What you thought was a garage was a Japanese bathhouse."

"I want to go home," Michael said in a whiny voice.

"He's so tired," Janey's mother said, talking more to herself than to anyone else as she put the car in gear and eased forward when the line inched ahead.

CHAPTER ELEVEN

"Get parked and get out!"

Coming out of the darkness with no warning at all, the shout startled Janey. She glared at the soldier, but he was already gone, moving down the line of cars to instruct the drivers behind them. Janey waited for her mother to park, then got out slowly. Akiko joined her, standing close. Janey could feel her trembling. Michael was half asleep, and Mom lifted him out of the Buick.

"Let's go! Move along now!"

Janey couldn't see who was ordering them to hurry, but she felt Akiko flinch in reaction to the rough, impatient voice.

"Maybe they have something we can eat," Janey heard her mother say. "If they feed me, they can yell at me the rest of the night and I won't care."

Janey smiled, but she could see that Akiko was tense and frowning as they started forward, the sandy soil gritting beneath their shoes. There were cars parked in makeshift rows all around them.

An odd sound from somewhere above them made Janey look up. "What was that?"

"A *pueo*," Akiko said. "An owl."

Janey let out a long breath. "We have barn owls at home. Pueo. Is that Japanese for 'owl'?"

Akiko shook her head. "Hawaiian."

"It's too dark," Michael complained quietly.

"This way, please, folks." The next soldier's politeness made Janey smile at him as they passed. He smiled at her, too, then she saw his face stiffen a little when he noticed Akiko. A smile replaced the look of surprise almost immediately, and Janey hoped that Akiko hadn't seen it at all. She was scared enough.

"Right in this way," a third soldier said, directing people with a repetitive wave of one hand, like a policeman directing traffic. Janey hooked her arm through Akiko's and walked close behind her mother as they followed a path around the side of the building to wide double doors. There were overhead lights, but only the one farthest from the door had been turned on.

"Is there food?" asked a woman coming in just behind them.

"I forgot the poi," Akiko said suddenly.

"Of course. I should have thought to have you bring it," Janey's mother said, turning around. "Wait here with your sister. I'll be right back, sweetie," she told Michael, bending to set him down beside Janey. She steadied him; he really was sleepy.

"Kaikamahine?"

Akiko turned to face the woman behind them. She was tall and had beautiful eyes. She was carrying two small children, one on each hip. They were both dozing against her shoulders.

"What did she say?" Janey whispered to Akiko.

Akiko glanced at her. "Just 'girl'—she just wanted my attention," Akiko whispered back. Then she looked up into the woman's face. "Yes, ma'am?"

"I heard you say you have poi? Enough to share? We have some sausages and rice we could give you."

Akiko nodded. "I have a big jar of it . . . and none of us really likes it much." She looked at Janey. Janey nodded eagerly. As hungry as she was, eating poi still sounded icky. Sausage sounded good enough to make her mouth water. The woman said something else that Janey couldn't hear, then turned to talk to a teenage boy standing behind her.

The murmuring conversations in the room were getting louder. Janey looked around. There were at least a hundred people in the building, she thought, maybe more. At the far end of the room she could see a soldier gesturing broadly, getting people to choose a place along the walls to sit or lie down on the floor.

There was a stack of blankets on a table, and people were milling around them. Janey glanced at the door and saw her mother coming in, carrying the poi jar and an old blanket Janey's father had put in the trunk of the car for his early morning surf-fishing ventures.

Within an hour, most of the people were settled in and had eaten something. The plantation owner's family had made huge pots of rice and beans. Many of the people from the cane fields had brought at least some food—most of which was shared. A man who had been hauling a truckload of pineapples to a Honolulu market when the attack began cut the ripest fruits and passed out the slices to all who wanted it. As soon as they'd eaten, Janey's mother spread their blanket on the floor, and Michael fell asleep on it.

The man with the radio set it up in a corner, and as the evening wore on, most of the adults drifted over to listen. Janey followed her mother and found a place to stand, leaning against the wall. Akiko sat beside Michael as he slept, her knees up and her arms crossed over them.

The radio volume varied, and the speaker squealed at times, then shattered into painfully loud static. But when people could hear voices, they all leaned closer, trying to make out what was being said. Some of the broadcasts were local, and announcers were telling people to report to work if they had government jobs. Other broadcasts, from farther away, seemed vague and unsure about what had happened. People whispered to those behind them what they had heard.

It was obvious to Janey that no one really knew what was going on. One announcer said that San Diego,

California had been invaded, but then another man said Hawaii was the only place that had been attacked so far.

"The corporal as much as told me that Honolulu was being attacked," a man standing near Janey said loudly.

"We were told the same thing," she said, but her voice was tight and small, and no one heard her.

"You are scaring the children," a woman scolded him. The man mumbled an apology and fell silent. Everyone went back to trying to hear the shortwave radio. Janey slipped forward to get closer.

All the radio broadcasters speculated how many Japanese planes had been involved, where they had come from, and why they hadn't been detected sooner. The announcers all wondered what President Roosevelt would do. Everyone standing around the radio seemed to think there was no choice left but to go to war.

After a long time, some of the people around the radio gave up their places to those who'd had to stand farther away. Others refused to move away and stood silent and tense. When Janey's mother left, Janey followed her back across the room, not because she didn't want to hear more news from the announcers but because she was so tired, she nearly felt sick. She thought about Pokey and hoped she was asleep warm and safe under the porch. She thought about her father, too, then pushed the thoughts away. They hurt too much.

It was hard to make a place on the plank floor to sleep. There weren't enough blankets to go around. The plantation owner's family had shared what they could, and the families who lived on the farm and worked in the cane fields had helped out, too. But there were just too many people for any of them to be very comfortable that night: too many people and not enough bedding or room—and not enough answers.

Janey watched her mother spread out the two blankets they had been loaned alongside the one from their trunk. Michael was still sound asleep on it lying facedown like a baby, snoring lightly.

As they got ready to lie down, they were careful not to talk too loudly, as much for the people on either side of them as for Michael. Mom had also found two sweaters and a jacket in the trunk, to roll up for pillows.

"Michael is sound asleep," Akiko said in a low voice as Janey's mother moved him gently to make room for herself to lie down. "I wish I were."

"Me, too," Janey said. She heard the intensity in her own voice and wondered if Akiko felt the same way. She was so tired that she felt trembly, but she was almost sure she wouldn't be able to sleep. How could she? She had no idea if her father was all right. And there *was* going to be a war. "Okay, you two," Janey's mother said. "At least lie down and try to rest. We can't know how long it'll be before we can go home or what will happen, but being exhausted won't help anything tomorrow."

Akiko didn't answer, but she stretched out on the edge of the last blanket, scrunched over to take up as little room as possible. Janey lay down beside her, wriggling around to get her skirt straight.

Janey's mother reached out to pat her cheek, then she leaned over and kissed her on the forehead, then touched Akiko's hair lightly. "You two have been a big help all through this miserable long day," she said, sighing. "I just hope we can find our families tomorrow."

Janey heard the worry in her mother's voice and wondered if she was going to start crying. But she didn't. She just lay down beside Michael and closed her eyes. Akiko settled onto the blankets, too, a little sigh escaping her lips.

"Good night," Mom said quietly.

Akiko lifted her head. "Good night, Mrs. Blue."

"Good night," Janey echoed. Then she just concentrated on lying still. The floor was really *hard*. She could hear whispers and a woman crying, and the sound of a baby fussing. She had never before slept in a place with a hundred strangers in it. As it got quieter, as people settled down for the night, Janey could hear sounds from outside, too. The owl called over and over. After a long while, Janey realized that she was still listening for the distant sound of plane engines. She was afraid to stop.

CHAPTER TWELVE

A roaring explosion of big guns jerked Janey from sleep, and she stumbled to her feet, nearly falling over Akiko.

"What is it?" someone shouted in the darkness.

"Attack!" a man shouted back. "It's our guns firing. It must be the invasion!"

People stumbled upright, stunned and scared. Janey bit at her lower lip, turning one way, then the other. She could hear planes, she was sure of it, *planes*. "What should we do?" she asked her mother.

Mom had grabbed up Michael and now stood with him clutched against her. The sky that Janey could see through the big double doors was streaked with lights that flashed, then dimmed. The whole island of Oahu seemed to shake under the din of the guns. Janey covered her ears and sank to her knees. It was too much, it was just too much to stand. She felt someone taking her hands, then hugging her, and she opened her eyes to see Akiko in the half-light of the shed. Her mother was there a second later, holding Michael. They huddled, pressing close together, until the firing finally slowed, then stopped.

The silence was as strange for a moment as the gun-fire had been. From somewhere back toward Honolulu, a single burst of firing was heard, then the silence closed in again.

"Are they invading?" Akiko asked.

Janey's mother leaned back and rocked back and forth on her knees to soothe Michael's hysterical crying. "I don't know," she said finally. "Lie back down for now. There's nothing else we can do. Try to rest."

Janey waited until Akiko had settled herself again, then she stretched out beside her. Mom was lying on her back, with Michael still in her arms. Janey could hear her own heart pounding as she listened to the other people in the building discussing what to do. The buzzing static of the shortwave radio came to life, and she lifted her head to see a group of men at the back of the building again.

"Janey?"

She turned. "What, Akiko?"

"I will be your best friend here. Tilly is still your best friend in Kansas, of course."

Janey felt hot tears trickling sideways from the outer corners of her eyes and rolling downward to soak into her dress collar.

"I didn't mean to make you cry," Akiko said softly.

Janey reached out blindly and found Akiko's hand, unable to say anything at all.

Mom cleared her throat. "Janey? Are you all right?"

"Yes," Janey managed to say, but she held Akiko's hand tightly and tried to stop crying. It took a long time.

It was the longest night in history, Janey thought. No one slept, she was sure. And she was not the only one who cried off and on in the hours before dawn. She did manage to do it quietly—something everyone tried to do, it seemed like. Akiko was one of the quietest criers in the world. She made so little noise that Janey didn't know she was crying until she sniffled a little and used her free hand to wipe at her eyes.

People began stirring as soon as the sky lightened in the east. Janey sat up, her back aching from the hard floor. Akiko propped herself up, too, yawning. Janey saw her mother's eyelids flutter and knew she wasn't asleep. "Will they let us go home now?" Janey whispered, knowing that her mother didn't know, but asking anyway.

"Shhh," Mom whispered. "You'll wake Michael. He only went to sleep about half an hour ago. See what the radio is saying, if you can."

Janey nodded and gestured to Akiko. They made their way through the people lying on the floor to the back of the room where fifteen or twenty men circled the radio. The man who owned it was fiddling with the dials. There was static—worse now than the night before—and bits and pieces of broadcasts that were repeating what they had heard yesterday.

When they went back to tell Janey's mother, she

was sitting up and Michael was rubbing at his eyes. "I think we should try to get home," she said very quietly. "We'll just find your father, then come back up here."

"Will they let us leave?" Akiko asked.

Janey watched her mother frown. "We can try to see. Don't make a fuss, just follow me out. Leave the blankets here. We'll be back."

Janey's heart began to thump hard in her chest again. The idea of trying to fool the soldiers scared her, but not nearly as much as another day of wondering whether her father was all right.

No one was outside the doors as they stepped into the pink-sky morning. Three or four men were already standing beside their cars. They had government jobs, Janey realized, as they backed out and pulled away.

"Hurry," Janey's mother said as they got into the car. "Everyone get in front." She shoved the key into the ignition. "Put Michael between you. And sit still and stay down."

Janey held her breath as they pulled out of the rows of parked cars—but no one stopped them. Mom drove fast, but not too fast, staying behind the men's cars as they came down out of the mountains and turned onto the government road and headed for Pearl City. Janey tried to see out, but the smoke from the harbor was still rising, drifting over the peninsula, and she couldn't spot their house. She saw her mother looking, too, her eyes narrowed.

There were jeeps on the road that morning. Janey could watch them, inching herself up just enough to see over the dashboard. "Get your head down," Mom said tensely. Then she drove onward, her chin jutting out and her eyes looking straight ahead. The soldiers glanced up and let her pass.

After a few more tense seconds, they rounded a bend in the road and Mom grinned as they all clapped. Michael smiled brightly, and Janey knew he had no idea what had just happened, but it didn't matter. She hugged him and exchanged a smile with Akiko as they slowed to go through Pearl City, passing the stores and the theater again. Nothing was damaged, as far as Janey could see. The sunny morning seemed strange and out of place.

Their house looked normal too, and the car parked slantwise on the edge of the road was the only thing that jarred Janey's nerves as they approached. It was eerie, the silence of the morning as they got out of the car.

"Check your house, please, Akiko. If your parents are there, tell them they may certainly come with us if they want to." Mom reached out and touched Akiko's cheek. "If they're not, you'll stay with us and we'll find them later."

Akiko nodded, and Janey tried to smile at her, but her mouth was twisted with worry. She stood, eyeing their closed front door, trying to imagine her father behind it, still asleep, about to be startled and over-joyed when his family arrived.

"Come on." Mom pulled in a long breath and squared her shoulders as she picked Michael up. Janey followed her up the walk. Halfway to the door, Pokey appeared from beneath the porch, and Janey dropped to her knees to hug the wriggling little dog. "We'll take her with us this time," Mom said, but she didn't shorten her stride, and Janey jumped to her feet to follow her through the kitchen door.

"Jack?" Mom called. "Honey, are you here?"

There was no answer, and Janey balled her hands into fists. "Daddy?"

Silence greeted them as they went from the kitchen to the living room, leaving the door standing open behind them. Janey saw her mother's note on the radio. Michael's toys were on the floor. Janey heard her brother make a whimpering sound as they went through the house, checking the bedrooms. Then Mom cleared her throat. "I'll leave another note, that's all. We'll come every day to check, and we'll go into Honolulu as soon as we can and—"

"Janey? Mrs. Blue?" It was Akiko's voice, soft and polite as always, coming from the kitchen door. Janey's heart sank. Akiko's parents must not be there, either. How could they stand this? How could anyone stand this kind of worry?

"I'll write the note," Mom said. She set Michael down. "Take your brother, honey, and I'll be right there."

Janey stared at her mother for a second. Her voice

was level and calm, but her hands were shaking as she turned on the radio. Janey took Michael's hand and led him back into the kitchen. She heard the sound of the warming radio tubes crackling behind her.

"Look," Akiko said as Janey came into the kitchen. She stepped aside and pointed. Janey blinked and stood still. There, coming up the steps with Akiko's parents helping him walk slowly toward her, was her father.

"Mom?" Janey said, but her voice was breathy and ragged. She turned toward the living room as Michael pushed past her and ran toward Dad. "Mom? He's here. He's here!"

Seconds later they all stood in the living room. Music swelled softly from the radio, and Janey felt like she was in a movie, with the happiest ending anyone could have hoped for. Akiko's parents' eyes were shining and her mother kept touching her, then exchanging long looks with her husband.

Janey hugged her father. He smelled of oil and soot, and she was scared about him being hurt. But his arms around her felt strong and solid, and she started crying. "I have a bad cut on one leg, Janey, that's all. I was lucky. And Mrs. Fujiwara cleaned and dressed the wound. I lost a lot of blood, but I feel stronger every second. Seeing all of you . . ." He trailed off and straightened up, turning to embrace Janey's mother.

Janey watched her parents embrace, then Mom stepped back and burst into tears. Michael stood beside his father, refusing to move even when Daddy nearly fell over him trying to get to the couch. Sitting side by side, her parents began talking in low voices, Mom explaining about the plantation building, the soldiers that had turned her back, her father saying only a little about the attack on Hickam Field.

"My parents walked back home," Akiko told Janey. "But they crossed the fields and stayed off the road because they thought an invasion would come. They are most grateful to your mother for caring for me."

"I'm grateful your mother was here to help my dad," Janey said.

Akiko's mother asked her a question in Japanese, and Akiko answered. Then Mrs. Fujiwara turned to Janey. "My daughter says you are good friends now."

Janey nodded. "We are." Then she took a breath, meaning to thank the Fujiwaras for helping her father, but suddenly the music stopped, and an announcer introduced the president of the United States, Franklin Delano Roosevelt. They all fell silent and faced the radio.

"Yesterday, December 7, 1941—a date which will live in infamy—the United States of America was suddenly and deliberately attacked by naval and air forces of the Empire of Japan," the president said grimly.

"The United States was at peace with that nation and, at the solicitation of Japan, was still

in conversation with its Government and its Emperor looking toward the maintenance of peace in the Pacific. Indeed, one hour after Japanese air squadrons had commenced bombing in Oahu, the Japanese Ambassador to the United States and his colleague delivered to the Secretary of State a formal reply to a recent American message. While this reply stated that it seemed useless to continue the existing diplomatic negotiations, it contained no threat or hint of war or armed attack.

"It will be recorded that the distance of Hawaii from Japan makes it obvious that the attack was deliberately planned many days or even weeks ago. During the intervening time the Japanese Government had deliberately sought to deceive the United States by false statements and expressions of hope for continued peace.

"The attack yesterday on the Hawaiian Islands has caused severe damage to American naval and military forces. Very many American lives have been lost. In addition American ships have been reported torpedoed on the high seas between San Francisco and Honolulu.

"Yesterday the Japanese Government also launched an attack against Malaya.

"Last night Japanese forces attacked Hong Kong.

"Last night Japanese forces attacked Guam.

"Last night Japanese forces attacked the Philippine Islands.

"Last night the Japanese attacked Wake Island.

"Last night the Japanese attacked Midway Island.

"Japan has, therefore, undertaken a surprise offensive extending throughout the Pacific area. The facts of yesterday speak for themselves. The people of the United States have already formed their opinions and well understand the implications to the very life and safety of our nation.

"As Commander-in-Chief of the Army and Navy I have directed that all measures be taken for our defense.

"Always will we remember the character of the onslaught against us.

"No matter how long it may take us to overcome this premeditated invasion, the American people in their righteous might will win through to absolute victory."

Akiko's mother began to cry and Janey couldn't hear for a moment, but the meaning was clear enough. They were at war now. The president's voice rose, clear and loud.

"... I asked that the Congress declare that since the unprovoked and dastardly attack by Japan on Sunday, December seventh, a state of war has existed between the United States and the Japanese Empire."

Then President Roosevelt's voice stopped, and there was only crackling static. Janey's father turned to Akiko's parents. "My wife knows the way to an evacuation center. We should probably all go, as quickly as we can." Mr. Fujiwara nodded, a quick jerking motion, ignoring his wife's frown.

Janey felt her father's hand on her shoulder. "Get your pajamas and your toothbrush, and pack a bag like you were going to a slumber party back home, honey."

Janey started for her room, her feelings a tangle that she knew would not be sorted out for a long time—maybe never. Her country was at war. It sounded like something out of a history book, not something that should be happening now. But her father was safe and so were her mother and brother, and even Pokey. Out her bedroom window Janey saw Akiko running ahead of her parents back to their house. She opened the window a crack and listened. Silence.

"Hurry!" her father called.

"I am," Janey answered, and turned to her nightstand to get her diary.

December 9, 1941 Refugee Camp, Oahu:

It's early again. No one really sleeps yet, we all just doze and listen. They are calling us refugees now. And they are saying that Honolulu was not invaded, so Akiko feels better about her relatives there.

What a strange time this is; I know I will remember it forever. Akiko's mother is still nervous, and I do see some of the people looking at Akiko's father sidelong, watching him. He says he will prove his patriotism to his neighbors, to anyone who questions it. I think this war is going to be awful, in every way.

Daddy says we can only be as brave as we can be and get through it. A medic looked at his wound today and said it is healing and not infected. He also said that Mrs. Fujiwara cleaned it as well as a doctor would have. Daddy said it hurt so much that he figured she'd done a good job. They laughed. Everyone laughs at little things now, even me and Akiko. We played hopscotch yesterday with some other girls and we laughed like crazy. But then we all got quiet and listened for a few seconds. So far, there are no more planes.